A Bite-Sized Environment Book

Exploring the Green Economy
Issues, Challenges, and Benefits

Edited by

Beverley Nielsen & Steve McCabe,
Institute of Design, Economic Acceleration, and
Sustainability (IDEAS), Birmingham City University

Cover by

Dean Stockton

Published by Bite-Sized Books Ltd 2021

Bite-Sized Books Ltd 8th Floor, 20 St Andrew Street, London, England, EC4A 3AG

team@bite-sizedbooks.com

Registered in the UK. Company Registration

No: 9395379

Contents

PART ONE
What are the Fundamentals of a Greener Economy?

PART TWO
Principles in Action

Acknowledgments

In coordination and editing a book dedicated to the subject of the green economy, we are acutely aware of the magnitude and importance of the subject. The need for all societies in all parts of the world to become 'greener' in approaches to living, working and economic progression is accepted by all but diehard climate change sceptics. It is now no longer a matter of what needs to be done but how quickly. Achieving change requires, of course, action which can only happen by coordinated intervention and altered behaviour by everyone from government to individuals.

Consistent with the aspirations of Bite-Sized Books, this text is intended to provide an overview of what developing a green economy consists of. As such we have endeavoured to cover a broad spectrum of issues. Consequently, whilst we may be accused of not having incorporated everything that is crucial, we have striven to include what we regard as the critical aspects of the theory and, equally importantly, practice of implementation of a green economy.

As such this text includes contributions from authors explaining what's involved and how positive change leading to a greener economy can be facilitated. It has been completed with profound gratitude to those who've dedicated time and effort to this task. Without their involvement this book would not have the range of opinion and diversity which, we hope, makes it worth reading.

Beverley Nielsen and Dr Steven McCabe, July 2021

Foreword

The Baroness Brown of Cambridge, Professor Dame Julia King DBE FREng FRS, formerly Deputy Chair, Climate Change Committee (CCC), Chair CCC Adaptation Committee; Chair of the Carbon Trust and Non-Executive Director of renewable energy company Ørsted and of fuel cell and electrolyser company Ceres Power

In considering how we can meet environmental targets, crucial to delivering Net Zero and fulfilling our commitments to the Paris Agreement, and in the context of the fact that we are holding the COP26 Climate Conference later this year, we must now focus on action and on increasing the pace of our response.

The challenge ahead is immense. Whilst it has been heartening to see Parliament addressing this with urgency, we must not lose this focus, given the many other pressing challenges we face. Whilst I was Deputy Chair of the Climate Change Committee (CCC), following our recommendations for the UK to achieve net zero emissions by 2050, the Climate Change Act was amended in the fastest implementation of a recommendation by the CCC in its 10 year lifetime. The Government has now gone on to accept the CCC's recommendations on the level of the 6th Carbon Budget and the inclusion of international aviation and shipping. However, actions have not kept pace with intentions and the failure to address the threat posed by climate change is resulting in changes to our climate that will make the lives of millions, particularly those whose existence is already precarious, considerably worse. In the UK, we are already experiencing the impact of climate change and the latest work of the CCC shows that we are woefully unprepared as things stand with too many in government appearing to put off adaptation until tomorrow and failing to recognise that the time for urgent action is now.

It is essential every organisation, from government outwards, as well as each of us as individuals, is committed to supporting action to limit further climate change from greenhouse gas emissions, and to adapt to the inevitable changes that are already locked-in to the system. The way in which we live, work, enjoy our leisure, must all be considered in the context of impact on the environment and the changes in climate still to come. Improvement can only be delivered through collective action, with strong leadership from government. That action must explicitly recognise the fragility of our planet and the importance of urgent action if we are to preserve a viable future for the generations to come.

The CCC estimates that around 60% of the emissions reduction needed to achieve Net Zero in the UK, and to halt our contribution to the changing climate, involves some level of behaviour change. We need to commit to making those changes, just as business needs to commit to delivering zero carbon products and services, to ensure our children and grandchildren can enjoy at least the quality of life and diversity of nature we ourselves have enjoyed.

I welcome this book as a positive contribution to developing a green economy. I hope that those who read it will be inspired to take action.

About the editors

Beverley Nielsen is Executive Director and Associate Professor at the Institute for Design, Economic Acceleration & Sustainability *(IDEAS)* as well as a Senior Fellow within the Centre for Brexit Studies, both based at Birmingham City University. Beverley chairs Ultra Light Rail Partners Ltd, responsible for developing biomethane-powered lightweight trains and trams, having previously been awarded Innovate UK and Department for Transport development grants. She serves as an Expert Commissioner for the All-Party Parliamentary Group on Manufacturing and has recently co-edited two books including *English Regions After Brexit* with Dr Steve McCabe and *Brexit Negotiations After Article 50* with Professor Alex de Ruyter, having also co-written *Redesigning Manufacturing* with economist, Vicky Pryce and Professor Michael Beverland. She is an Independent Councillor representing Malvern on Worcestershire County and Malvern Hills District Councils.

Dr Steven McCabe is Associate Professor at the Institute for Design, Economic Acceleration & Sustainability *(IDEAS)* and Senior Fellow within the Centre for Brexit Studies, both of which are based at Birmingham City University. Steven is a long-standing academic and has written extensively on issues of management, business and politics. In the last two years, as well as writing a number of chapters dealing with Brexit, inequality and the pandemic, he has co-edited *Brexit and Northern Ireland, Bordering on Confusion* (published by Bite-Sized Books, ISBN-13:978-1694447807) and *English Regions After Brexit: Examining Potential Change through Devolved Power* (also published by Bite-Sized Books, ISBN-13: 979-8666953099).

Chapter One

Introduction – Crisis, what crisis and why developing a green economy is critical to collective survival?

Dr Steven McCabe and Beverley Nielsen, IDEAS, BCU Birmingham

There's a storm brewing!

Search any newspaper or media website and it's almost certain the word 'green' will appear. In recent years the public might be forgiven for believing they're being bombarded with the message that becoming greener in everything we do is imperative. The reason, we're informed, is because of a phenomenon known as global warming. This, it's explained, is an identifiable trend that, because of the burning of fossil fuels, has become more pronounced in recent decades. The burning of fossil fuel by humanity, occurring from many millennia ago as a way to keep warm and cook, has risen dramatically since the industrial revolution when, in Britain, coal was used to create energy to operate machines in factories. Coal, formed by dead plant matter that was converted by heat and pressure into the black or brown-black sediment we're familiar with over millions of years, burns hot and consistently. As such, coal was ideal to heat water to create steam to operate the rapidly developing machines making mass produced goods, the central objective of the industrialisation.

Burning coal, however, produces emissions which, because of its origins, are largely carbon dioxide though sulphur, nitrogen and hydrogen are also emitted. Whilst the amount of coal used for fuel in Great Britain is vastly less than a generation ago, because it is cheap to mine, it still provides approximately a third of the world's power according to Greenpeace (2021). This is particularly so in the case of large developing nations such as China and India, The UK, similar to all developed and mature economies, has switched to oil and gas. Though less 'dirty' than coal, oil and gas because of being formed by dead marine organisms which were subject to heat and pressure over millions of years (National Geographic, 2019), still create emissions including high levels of carbon dioxide.

Global Emission of Carbon Due to Fossil Fuels – 1900-2014 (Source: Boden, Marland and Andres, 2017)

The consequence is that, since the industrial revolution, which commenced in the mid eighteenth century, enormous amounts of the trace elements from burning coal, oil and gas have been released. This, in turn, has caused a notable increase in what's known as 'greenhouse gases' which have the effect of trapping heat within the earth's atmosphere and, significantly, causing the average temperature of earth to increase.

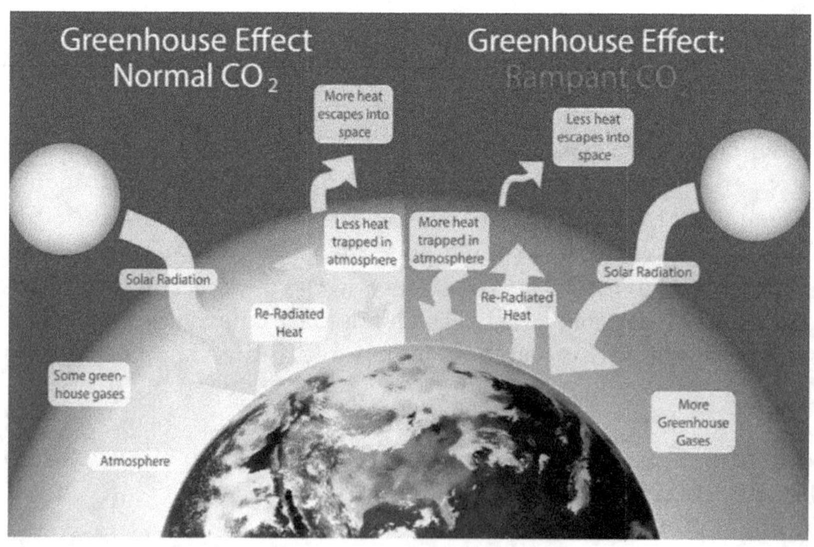

In 2020, fossil fuels were responsible for 84% of the energy generated across the globe. Influential global organisation, the Intergovernmental Panel on Climate Change (IPCC), stress that this means greenhouse gases will continue to rise, which, in turn, adds to the potential risk for global warming to occur. However, the needs of humanity and our voracious exploitation of minerals as well as land to produce food, is adding to greenhouse gases. As the chart below shows, carbon dioxide (CO_2), represents 76% of greenhouse gases. Methane (CH_4) is created by 'intensive' agricultural practices, waste management, energy use and biomass burning. Though CH_4 accounts for 16% of greenhouse gases, it is 34 times more harmful over a 100-year period than CO_2 (Houghton, Jenkins and Ephraums, 1990). Nitrous oxide (N_2O), making up 6% of greenhouse gases, is produced by burning fossil fuels and fertilizer use in agriculture. The remainder of greenhouse gases, 2%, are fluorinated, synthetic F-gases, which originate from industrial processes, refrigeration as well as a variety of consumer products creating hydrofluorocarbons (HFCs), perfluorocarbons (PFCs), and sulphur hexafluoride (SF_6).

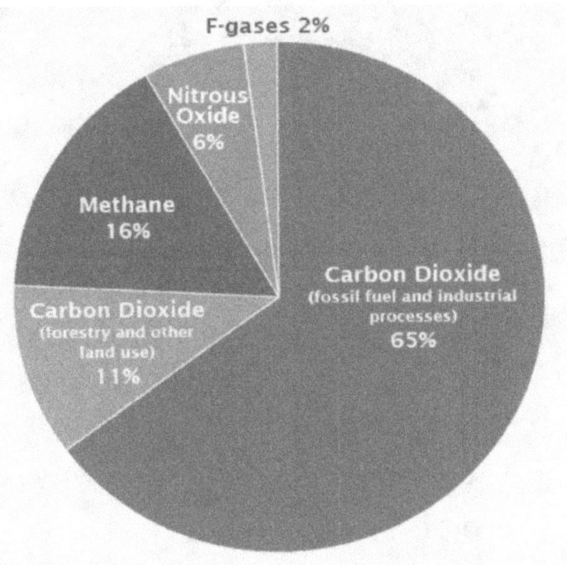

Global Emission of Greenhouse Gases (Source: IPCC, 2014)

Greenhouse gases and their destructive impact

As anyone who's been in a greenhouse when the sun shines will experience, it can become very hot and uncomfortable. Unless air is allowed into the greenhouse to cool it, the heat will be so intense as to potentially kill plants. There will, of course, be relief from darkness. Though comparing the earth to a greenhouse may be limited, the earth's complex interactive weather and ecosystems notwithstanding, the impact of a continually rising temperature, caused by greenhouse gases, is not dissimilar. A rising average temperature for the earth will lead to disruption of naturally occurring cycles that have allowed life, particularly humanity, to flourish. Notably, as the earth becomes warmer, more water vapour can be contained in the atmosphere. Effectively, water vapor acts as a greenhouse gas and increased water absorbs more heat contributing to further warming and creating a vicious cycle.

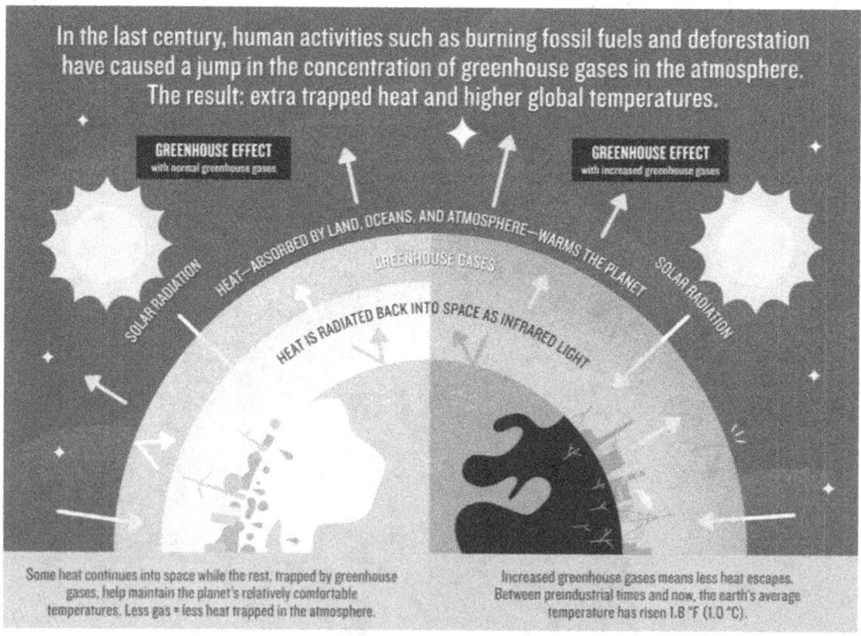

Source: NRDC (National Resources Defense Council)

The long-term average temperature of the earth, compared to pre-industrialisation, has increased by over 1°C. This trend has become marked in the last five decades (Shukman, 2021). Prior to industrialisation, in what's the Holocene Epoch, the 11,650 years since the last ice age, during which human civilisation developed, natural greenhouse gases in earth's atmosphere were between 200 and 280 parts per million. This ensured the ambient average temperature of our planet to be 15°C. However, greenhouse gases are causing this long-term average for earth to increase. As the chart presented below indicates, six studies provide evidence of the increase in the earth's average temperature.

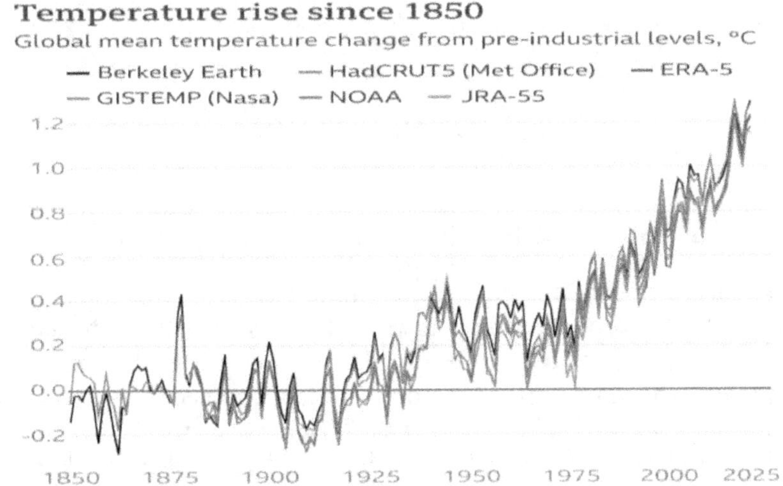

Source: Shukman/BBC (2021) based on Meteorological Office data

Crucially, without such natural gases this would be a frozen planet without life. Industrialisation combined with exponential population increase has resulted in a concentration of greenhouse gases well over 400 parts per million which has caused the rise in the earth's average temperature. As enshrined in the United Nations Climate Change 'Paris Agreement', a legally binding international treaty on climate change adopted by 196 Parties at COP 21 on 12th December 2015, unless the long-term rise in average global temperature is limited to below 2°C (and preferably 1.5°C, compared to the pre-industrial level, potential devastation will be impossible to avert.

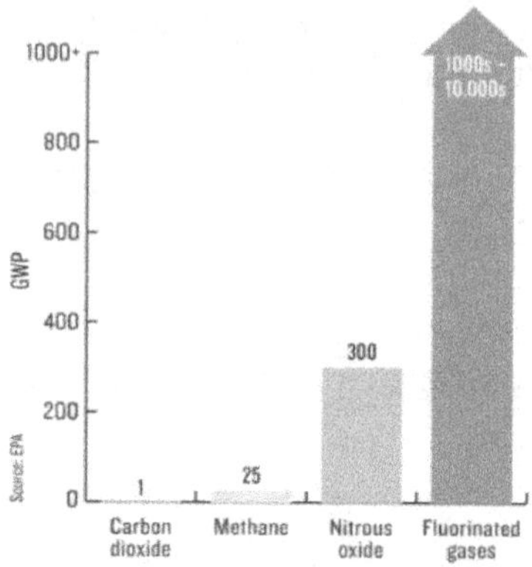

The global warming potential (GWP) of human-generated greenhouse gases is a measure of how much heat each gas traps in the atmosphere, relative to carbon dioxide.

Source: Denchak, (2019)

What could this mean for humanity?

Though human beings are believed to have emerged around 800,000 years ago, the level of damage the planet has suffered in the last 70 years is so great as to warrant an alternative era. What's known as the Anthropocene (human-centred) Epoch is characterised by the increase in greenhouse gases which, as we've experienced in the last 30 years, has resulted in extreme temperatures and weather patterns across the globe. As David Carrington, writing in the Guardian (2016) explains, human activity in the Anthropocene Epoch, as well as increasing C02 levels to the highest level in 66 million years, has additionally, increased extinction rates, now running at well above the long-term average. Carrington also explains that levels of plastic and microplastic particles in waterways and the sea are "now virtually ubiquitous" with attendant risks to long-term health.

The world's population has inexorably increased in the last 200 years, rising from 1 billion to currently, in excess of 7.8 billion. As a direct consequence there's been a corresponding rise in use of fossil fuel and consumption of the earth's resources. Growth in population, requiring continued prolific consumption of energy, food, and a vast range of minerals essential in building everything we use each day, is harmful and utterly destructive to planet earth. Humanity's 'success' in survival and multiplication is, ironically, leading to the destruction of the only known planet in the universe capable of supporting life.

Global warming, if allowed to continue unchecked, will make life considerably more difficult for many hundreds of millions of people who will be affected by climate change. Increasing temperature will result in greater prevalence of even more extreme weather than has already been experienced in recent years. Flooding, hurricanes, heat waves and droughts are likely to become commonplace. Habitation and survival for many, especially those whose lives are already blighted by poverty, will be an even greater challenge (Carrington, 2019). Fresh water will be in short supply for many (Harvey, 2020; Carrington, 2021). Melting ice caps will mean less land available and raised sea temperatures will create further problems for those, who, frequently, are among the poorest on earth (Milman, 2021). What the world's population faces because of climate change is irrevocably altered ecosystems and natural habitats that will potentially affect all life on the planet.

What Can be done?

Faced with impending catastrophe, action is urgently required.

It is imperative that radical reduction in emissions of greenhouse gases is central to whatever processes are carried out in the future. Every facet of our existence has an impact on the environment. Greenhouse gases, regardless of their origin, impact on the planet as a whole.

Though action by every individual is to be applauded, unless matched by collective endeavour across the globe, arresting the worst effects of climate change will not succeed.

As the following diagram indicates, though CO_2 is emitted in every part of the globe, some countries are more responsible for greenhouse gases than others.

China, whilst producing 30% of the world's CO_2, exports just under 20% of its GDP (World Bank 2021), indicating that the desire of global consumers (and governments) to purchase cheap goods is directly contributing to climate change.

This, arguably offers the most immediate thing we can collectively do to reduce greenhouse gas; reduce consumption.

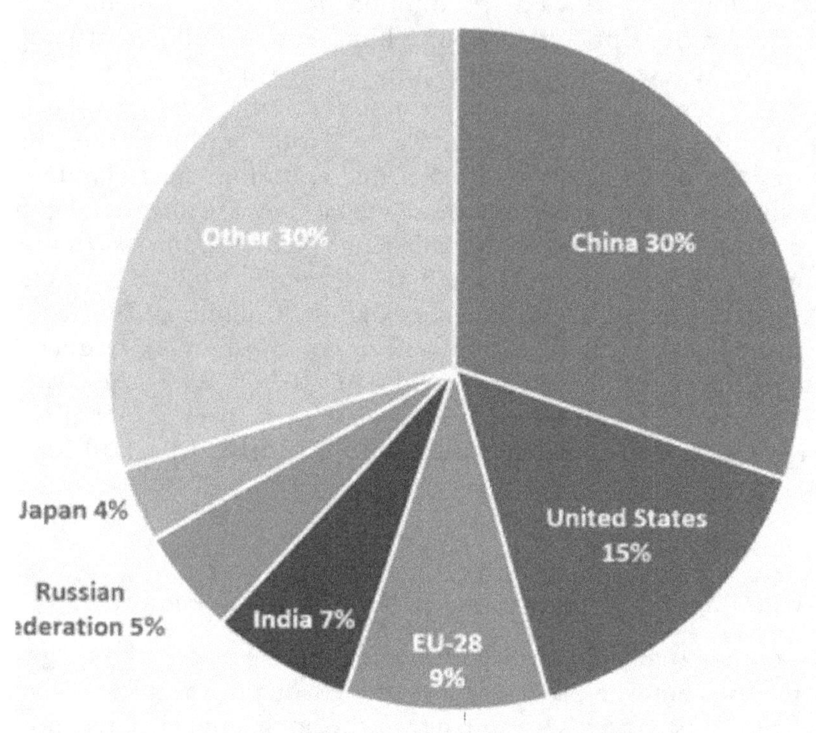

Emission of C0₂ by Country in 2014 (Source: Boden, T.A., Marland, G., and Andres, R.J., 2017)

In terms of activities and processes undertaken in any country, there will be variations in their level of contribution to greenhouse emissions. Usefully, IPCC, based on data collected in 2010, present averages for global emission of greenhouse gas for six key activities:

- Electricity and Heat Production (25%)
- Agriculture, Forestry, and Other Land Use (24%)
- Industry (21%)
- Transportation (14%)
- Other energy (10%)
- Buildings (6%)

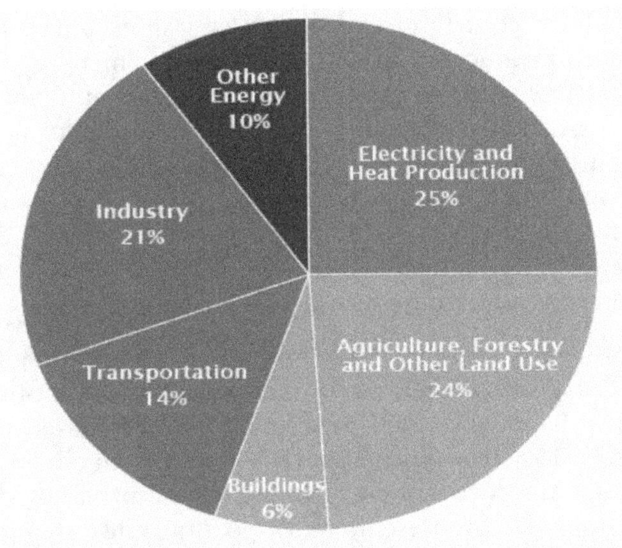

Global Emission of Greenhouse Gases by Sector (Source: IPCC, 2014)

In improving the level of greenhouse gases each of these activities provides opportunity for change. Though not easy or cheap, the scale of the catastrophe that will occur without immediate intervention means there is no choice. Delay will exacerbate the magnitude of the challenge and make the likelihood of calamity even greater. Crucially, all governments, organisations, businesses and, collectively, every individual, can play their part.

The largest contributory sector, Electricity and Heat Production, should be achieved using alternative sources which, as much as possible, are free from emission. Development of renewable energy by harnessing power from wind, solar and waves allow 'green' energy to be produced. Renewable energy is also possible through, for example, biomethane gas produced from organic waste.

Agriculture, forestry, and other land use, producing 24% of greenhouse gases, marginally less than electricity and heat production, must be carried out using methods of production that do not rely on the use of nitrogen-based fertilisers. Reducing consumption of meat and dairy products, which requires vast amounts of land to feed livestock, will be essential.

Industry, whose contribution through emissions is the most visible, should aim to produce, in the future, using green energy and with the explicit objective of elimination of waste and harmful emissions. This requires all of those engaged in industry (manufacturing) across the globe, in all parts of the supply chain, to redesign processes utilised. Such redesign will include extraction of raw materials and minerals through to distribution and delivery. As China's export data demonstrates, as consumers it's incumbent on us all to demand goods that have been made using green production methods.

Transportation, accounting for 14% global greenhouse gas emissions, includes all aspects of the way in which everything, both people and goods, move from one place to another. It's estimated that 90% of energy used for transport regularly used, which includes cars, motorcycles, vans, lorries, buses, trains, trains, airplanes and shipping, uses fossil fuel. This represents an opportunity for change leading to reduction in emissions through, for example, electric vehicles. Additionally, international trade and tourism comes at a cost which we should be fully aware of and seek to ameliorate.

Other energy, representing 10% of the greenhouse gases emitted, though not directly associated with electricity or heat production, incorporates fuel extraction, refining, processing, and transportation. These are areas which, as part of a coordinated effort by all countries, can be improved. Finally, buildings, essential for shelter and almost all activities that cannot be conducted outside, account for 6% of global greenhouse gas emissions through burning of energy, i.e. natural gas, to produce heat as well from cooking. Achieving reduction in greenhouse gas emissions from newly constructed buildings through improved design and alternative fuels is already underway. However, in any mature economy, such as the UK, the overwhelming majority of the 'built environment' already exists. Consequently, an ambitious programme known as 'retrofitting' and adaption is urgently required.

What's already underway?

As part of slowing down greenhouse gas emissions, all governments are committed to a reduction that will, initially, protect and, ultimately, restore the earth's atmosphere to levels consistent with stability of the climate. This is through adherence to the Paris Agreement, a legally binding international treaty on climate change, adopted by 196 Parties at COP 21 on 12th December 2015 and becoming binding on 4th November 2016. As part of an over-arching framework, the Paris Agreement provides financial, technical and capacity building support to any country requiring assistance.

The goal of this treaty is to limit global warming to below 2°C and, ideally, to 1.5 °C when compared with pre-industrial levels. The key objective is that by 2050, a climate neutral world is possible. As part of this objective, 'peak' greenhouse gas emission should occur as soon as possible and, thereafter, rapid reduction achieved.

Implementation of the Paris Agreement is based on economic and social transformation and operates on a five-year cycle of formulating ambitious climate change targets by all signatory countries. Countries submit plans of their intended action known as nationally determined contributions (NDCs). Additionally, consistent with the aspirations of the Paris Agreement, countries are invited to submit long-term low greenhouse gas emission development strategies (LT-LEDS). These, unlike NDCs, are not mandatory but ensure NDCs occur in the context of each country's long-term plans and priorities.

The Paris Agreement reaffirms that developed countries should take the lead in providing financial assistance to countries that are less endowed and more vulnerable, while for the first time also encouraging voluntary contributions by other Parties. Climate finance is needed for mitigation, because large-scale investments are required to significantly reduce emissions. Climate finance is equally important for adaptation, as significant financial resources are needed to adapt to the adverse effects and reduce the impacts of a changing climate.

A Rationale for Action – opportunities offered by developing a green economy

According to the UN Environmental Programme (2021), a green economy is defined as a "low carbon, resource efficient and socially inclusive". Such an economy is based on the desire to achieve growth in employment, as well as income, through investment by the public and public sectors. It is explicitly based on ensuring future investment in all aspects of economic activity is achieved without any further increase in greenhouse gases and with, correspondingly, reduced waste in activities carried out. Additionally, decreased pollution, enhanced energy and resource efficiency, as well as prevention of degradation of biodiversity and ecosystems, is regarded as fundamental to achieving a green economy.

As the UN stress, a green economy is not intended to replace sustainable development but, instead, deliberately focus on the economic opportunities possible. As such there are three strands (2021):

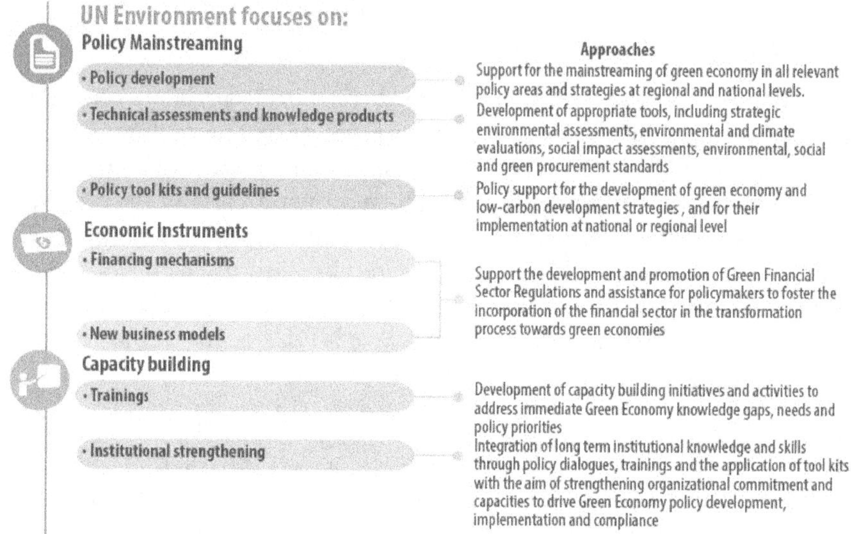

Source: UN Environmental Programme (2021)

According to the OECD (Organisation for Economic Co-operation and Development) in *Towards green growth, A summary for policy makers* (2011), any framework for green growth strategies must include the following two key objectives: improving resource management and boosting productivity; encouraging economic activity to take place where it is of best advantage to society over the long-term.

Both of these should be attained through innovation. This will require economic growth which will be based on institutional and individual investment decisions informed by the desire to produce a future that is green. As OECD recognise, "Advanced, emerging, and developing countries face different challenges and opportunities in greening growth, as will countries with differing economic and political circumstances." Creating a green economy will only be possible by the combination of policies implemented by government and incentives (financial or otherwise) provided to motivate a change in attitudes and behaviour.

Critical to success, OECD stress, is the connection between increased Gross Domestic Product (GDP) used to measure economic progress generally which enhances the importance of "natural assets to wealth, health and wellbeing". Equally critical, is that growth is beneficial to the health, wealth and welfare of all citizens in all parts of the world. This must include those who, traditionally, suffer greatest inequality and poverty in, most especially, developing countries. The location of natural assets in low-income countries means that green growth policies are highly likely to "reduce vulnerability to environmental risks and increase the livelihood security of the poor."

Consistent with the attainment of Millennium Development Goals (MDGs), OECD contend the following should be achieved: more efficient water, energy and transport infrastructure; alleviating poor health associated with environmental degradation; introducing efficient technologies that can reduce costs and increase productivity, while easing environmental pressure.

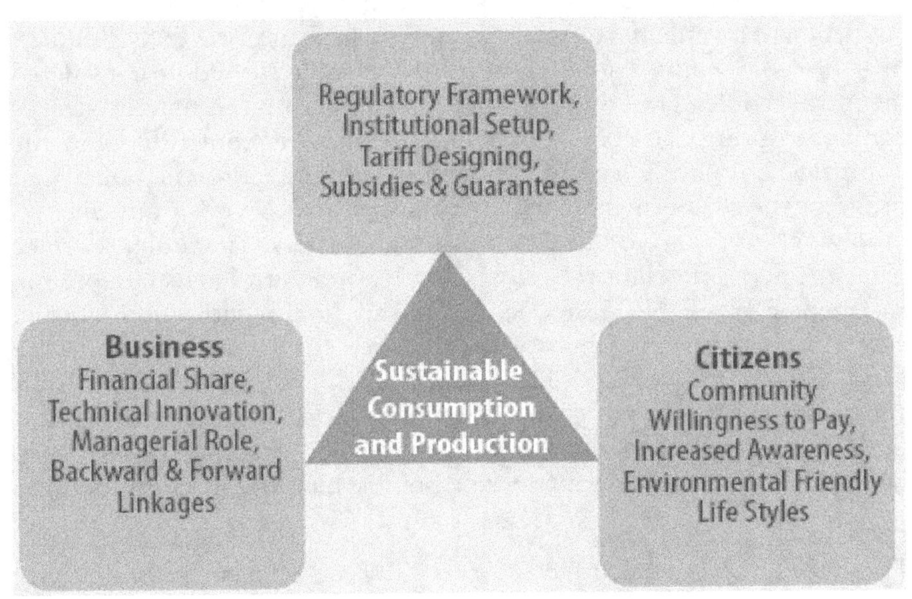

Source: UN Environmental Programme (2021)

What this book contains

The book is divided into two parts. The first, 'What are the Fundamentals of a Greener Economy?', is intended to consider how change leading to a green economy may be facilitated. In Chapter Two 'What do we think about developing a more circular economy? Rubbish!' Dr Steven McCabe examines the benefits of a circular economy. As he explains, re-use of items we currently dispose of will ensure a more virtuous cycle in which demand for raw materials is reduced. Using green energy will decrease pollution and greenhouse gases. In Chapter Three, 'Green economic models - what are they and how to accelerate?', seminal economist Vicky Pryce explores what alternative economic models consist of and how they can achieve 'greener' outputs. As Vicky believes, any argument that adopting such models may entail should be countered by the long-term benefits likely to accrue from "sustainably lower" expenditure produced by energy from renewables.

In Chapter Four, 'It's a sustainable economy, or it's no economy!' eminent environment campaigner and commentator, Tony Juniper, provides compelling argument as to why change should be considered incontrovertible. Drawing comparison from our recent experiences endured during the coronavirus pandemic he contends that the importance of nature as a fundamental aspect of economic policy and progress should be heightened. Jonathon Porritt, whose influence in moulding opinion on environmental matters, including Prince Charles', needs no elaboration. Stridently, and with his usual aplomb, in Chapter Five, 'No green economy can thrive without re-writing capitalism's rule book', he stresses the need for radical change in the way we approach economic policy and the environment. His conclusion, based on a quotation from Tim Jackson's recent book, *Post Growth, Life after Capitalism,* is that the "precepts of a Green Economy" should evolve into a rule book which becomes tomorrow's capitalism.

Tom Field, Chief Executive Officer, UVTech-Hygienics, in Chapter Six, 'Green entrepreneurship', provides explanation of what he believes to be the fundamentals that are necessary to achieve a greener approach to business by entrepreneurs. Using fascinating metaphors, Tom explicates the difference between 'green beans' and 'green machines'. Using innovation experience in his company, UVTech-Hygienics, he advises how entrepreneurs elsewhere can achieve similar achievements intended to inculcate green business as part of a wider effort to achieve a green economy.

The final contribution for Part One, Chapter Seven, 'Making a Just and Fair Transition Work for All', by Lisa Trickett and Bryan Nott, examines how interventions to avert climate change must garner support from across the spectrum of communities. As they cogently assert, it is essential that any changes are carried out in such a way as to support the sharing of potential benefits that may accrue. As such, Lisa and Bryan make a heartfelt plea that the 'resetting' of the economy that is needed in order to become green, is one in which structural changes explicitly address extant inequalities.

Addressing long-standing inequality, it should be stated, must be intrinsic to all initiatives developed by government and operationalised by every organisation. It is a principle that few can argue against. Recent events have demonstrated our world is based on an ever widening gap between those who have and those who have not. The impending catastrophe of climate change provides the opportunity to rebalance wealth and deal with the disparity that blights the lives of so many across the globe and, to be fair, in the UK. The notion of 'building back better' after the pandemic should aim to create a world that is radically improved for all.

Part Two of this book, 'Principles in Action' presents a number of chapters written by those who have engaged in achieving green initiatives in their organisations. In Chapter Eight, 'The implications of decarbonisation for regional identities: can the centre hold', Matthew Rhodes, Chair of West Midlands Energy Capital provides his views as to the importance of devolved decision-making on energy. Though, given the history of centralisation which exists in this country, Matthew is somewhat pessimistic that change will occur, he nonetheless provides persuasive arguments why such transition should occur.

In Chapter Nine, 'Growing Digital Economy and Connectivity for a Net Zero Age', Margot James, Chair of WMG, examines with Hopi Sen and Dr Vannessa Goodship, the potential for technological change to facilitate movement towards a state of 'net-zero' carbon in the UK. Through investment in the key components required to achieve this objective - infrastructure, materials, battery technology, data centres and a circular economy, Margot asserts embedding "green digitisation" is entirely achievable with the attendant benefits to all of us.

Tor Farquhar, Ex-HR Director, Tata Steel, Europe, in Chapter Ten, 'Building our Zero Carbon Economy on Green Foundations', describes how steel, crucial to our development as advanced societies, and equally critical to achieving green products of the future can be produced without producing additional carbon that's proved so detrimental to the environment. As Tor concludes in his contribution, success will be measured by a legacy in which the UK "becomes an exemplar of being the 'green workshop' of the world." David Seall, Independent Director, Advisor and Chartered Engineer, in Chapter Eleven, 'How the UK manufacturing sector can grasp the opportunities of new technologies and contribute to future sustainability', examines what is needed to underpin the transition to a green future by those who make goods as part of the British manufacturing sector. Critical to success, David contends, are updated skills, appropriate advice and technology and, of course, investment. The role of government, he argues, is key to industry producing in way conducive to a vastly improved environment.

In Chapter Twelve, 'What can we learn from a 2-year, £1mn Innovate UK 'Modern Methods of Construction' housing project', Richard Haynes, Franco Cheung and Paul Nicol examine what lessons have been gleaned from a project to build housing by whg Housing using a 'modern' approach that is highly innovative. This chapter demonstrates that considerable savings are possible including 33% reduction in life-cycle costs, 10% reductions in building costs, 50% reduction in design and construction time. Importantly, housing built using such methods allow occupiers to energy consumption "by at least 30%" and, critically for the environment, "carbon emissions [are] reduced by up to 50%".

In Chapter Thirteen, 'Biomethane, a Case Study based on Successful Circular Economy Practice', Beverley Nielsen examines how methane emissions, though in terms of proportion are lower than carbon, are far more destructive to the environment as a powerful greenhouse gas and can be harnessed to produce a green fuel. Biomethane, which Beverley suggests is not as well known or understood as it might be, may be used to provide an alternative fuel to petrol and diesel for transport. Using case studies, Beverley illustrates what has been achieved by Severn Trent plc.

In the final contribution to this book, Craig Sams, who co-founded Green & Black's and Carbon Gold, in Chapter Fourteen, 'Carbon Farming, A New and Profitable Crop for Farmers', presents compelling evidence of alternative methods for producing food than are currently utilised. As Craig contends with admirable passion, making a transition, based on fully appreciating the damage already inflicted on the planet through intensive farming practices and rapacious use of fertilizer is critical to creating a cleaner and greener future.

Craig believes that this will ensure an enhanced environment in which air quality is vastly improved, biodiversity encouraged, and our waterways and seas are purer. Craig's final comment, that the "end result will be the salvation of our beloved planet" serves as an abiding theme to what this book purports to achieve.

References

Boden, T. A.; Andres, R. J. and Marland, G. (2017), *Global, Regional, and National Fossil-Fuel CO2 Emissions (1751 - 2014)*, USDOE Office of Science (SC), Biological and Environmental Research (BER), United States

Carrington, D. (2016), 'The Anthropocene epoch: scientists declare dawn of human-influenced age', *The Guardian*, https://www.theguardian.com/environment/2016/aug/29/declare-anthropocene-epoch-experts-urge-geological-congress-human-impact-earth, 29th August, accessed 18th May

Carrington, D. (2019), 'Climate crisis seriously damaging human health, report finds', *The Guardian*, https://www.theguardian.com/environment/2019/jun/03/climate-crisis-seriously-damaging-human-health-report-finds, 3rd June, accessed 27th May

Carrington, D. (2021), 'Climate crisis is suffocating the world's lakes, study finds', *The Guardian*, **https://www.theguardian.com/environment/2021/jun/02/climate-crisis-is-suffocating-the-worlds-lakes-study-finds**, 2nd June, accessed 3rd June

Denchak, M. (2019), *Greenhouse Effect 101*, *https://www.nrdc.org/stories/greenhouse-effect-101#gases*, 16th July, accessed 14th May

Elder, W. (2021), What is Climate Change? https://www.nps.gov/goga/learn/nature/climate-change-causes.htm, accessed 25th May

Greenpeace (2021), Coal, https://www.greenpeace.org.uk/challenges/coal/, accessed 31st May

Harvey, F. (2020), 'More than 3 billion people affected by water shortages, data shows', *The Guardian*, https://www.theguardian.com/environment/2020/nov/26/more-than-3-billion-people-affected-by-water-shortages-data-shows, 26th November, accessed 22nd May

IPCC (2014), *Climate Change 2014 Mitigation of Climate Change Working Group III Contribution to the Fifth Assessment Report of the Intergovernmental Panel on Climate Change*, Cambridge University Press, Cambridge, UK

Houghton, J.T., Jenkins, G.J. and Ephraums, J.J. (1990), *Climate Change, The IPCC Scientific Assessment*, Cambridge University Press, Cambridge, UK

Milman, O. (2021), 'Global heating pace risks 'unstoppable' sea level rise as Antarctic ice sheet melts', *The Guardian*, https://www.theguardian.com/environment/2021/may/05/antarctica-ice-sheet-melting-global-heating-sea-level-rise-study, 5th May, accessed 6th May

National Geographic, (2019), *Fossil fuels, explained*, https://www.nationalgeographic.com/environment/article/fossil-fuels, accessed 17th May

OECD (2011), *Towards green growth, A summary for policy makers*, OEDC

Shukman, D. (2021), 'Climate: World at risk of hitting temperature limit soon', *BBC*, https://www.bbc.co.uk/news/science-environment-57261670, accessed 28th May

UN Environmental Programme (2021), Green Economy, https://www.unep.org/regions/asia-and-pacific/regional-initiatives/supporting-resource-efficiency/green-economy, accessed 22nd May

World Bank (2021), *Exports of goods and services (% of GDP) – China, https://data.worldbank.org/indicator/NE.EXP.GNFS.ZS?locations=CN*, accessed 8th June

Part One
What are the Fundamentals of a Greener Economy?

Chapter Two

What do we think about developing a more circular economy? Rubbish!

Dr Steven McCabe, Associate Professor, Institute of Design, Economic Acceleration & Sustainability (IDEAS), Birmingham City University

"The premise is simple: one economy and one environment, and they're interdependent." Dennis Weaver, (1924-2006), American actor and environmentalist advocate of alternative fuels and founder, in 1993, of the Institute of Ecolonomics

Overview

For a large proportion of the world's population, we live in a world of plenty. Goods and are available on demand. Provided we keep paying, we can continue to consume. However, such consumption has another less obvious cost. Our planet suffers the cost of depletion of natural resources required to make and transport goods. Fuel, essential in providing power to factories making things, our homes, places of work, for leisure, and the transport of goods and passengers, is a major contributor to environmental impact.

In their hugely detailed analysis, Intergovernmental Panel on Climate Change (IPCC) warned in its Fourth Assessment Report, *Climate Change 2007: Impacts, Adaptation and Vulnerability,* of the impending crisis climate change is producing for the earth. There will be severe impacts for significant parts of the world's population in terms of availability of water, ecosystems, food production, coastal erosion and health. As the diagram below clearly shows, since the late eighteenth century, there's been an exponential rise in the three 'greenhouse gases' of CO_2, CH_4, and N_2O:

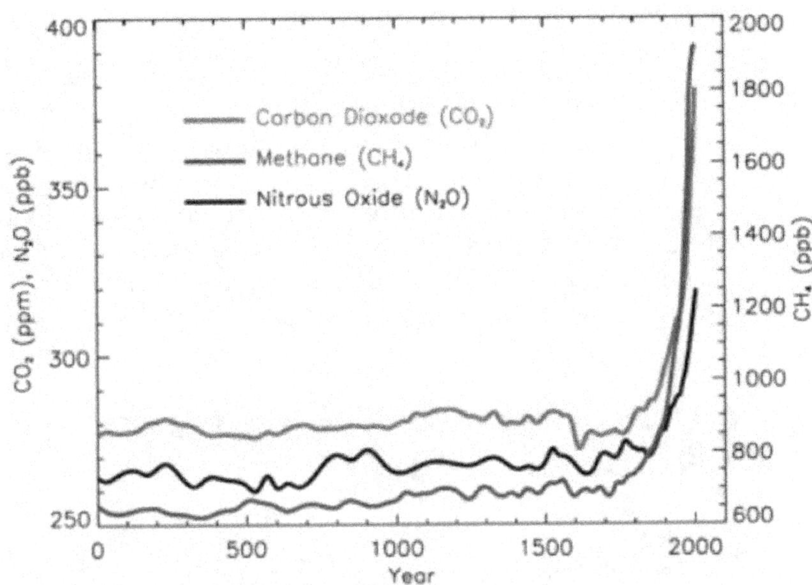

**Source: Intergovernmental Panel on Climate Change (IPCC) AR4
Frequently Asked Questions (2007)**

Mass production over the last 250 years, though making lives of those in developed nations collectively better, has resulted through greenhouse gas emissions, in trapping heat in the earth's atmosphere.

The planet is getting warmer.

Our consumption collectively contributes to an effect which, if unchecked, will have devastating consequences. Climate change, already causing raised temperatures, will continue to result in extreme weather, water shortages, melting ice caps and increased sea levels rising.

Those in the poorest countries will be most affected. As well as the potential loss of many millions of lives, habitation will be even more challenging than at present. Continued voracious consumption becomes an existential threat to humanity. Equally importantly, there's the challenge of what to do with the waste that's left when we've finished with items which, notably, have increasingly shorter effective life spans. Critics of the current system stress, there must be an alternative approach.

Reinventing 'Make do and mend'

My father, born between the two world wars, was of a generation which placed great value on items purchased. Even after something failed, he believed in cannibalising items for parts, screws, nails and other parts that might be used again. As such he adhered to the principle of 'make do and mend'. This was a slogan popularised by the Ministry of Information in 1943, as part of a campaign of rationing during the second world war. Citizens were exhorted to reuse, repair and repurpose items (Ministry of Information, 2007).

The character Mrs Sew and Sew, created to promote the Make Do and Mend campaign © IWM

Britain's wartime government was acutely aware of food shortages that had been rationed and available only through coupons.

In 1940 wastage of food became an offence. Unavoidable waste from food, such as skins of vegetables, was to be collected and used as feed for pigs.

Such measures, essential during the crisis of war, continued for a number of years after defeat of the Nazis. However, shortages faded.

We no longer worry about repair. Goods, often cheaper to replace than to mend, can be obtained at the touch of couple of buttons on computers and/or our mobile telephones. Besides, we're exhorted to have the latest version, model or style which change with alarming regularity.

Deliveries to our door are now standard. This is incredibly wasteful. As well as the discarded items, which must be disposed of, there is the vast amount of packaging any goods we receive are wrapped in.

It's estimated that an average household produces a tonne of waste each year, usually to landfill or to be incinerated. Some is recycled.

Data for waste disposal by local authorities in England is collected by DEFRA (Department for Environment, Food and Rural Affairs). As the diagram below shows, though recycling in England is currently just over 45%, a marked improvement to 2000, the rate of increase in the last decade has been much less impressive.

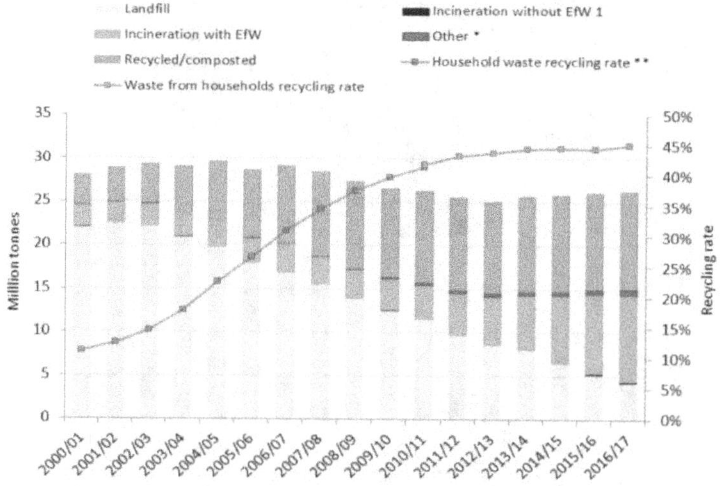

Management of all Local Authority collected waste and recycling rates in England, 2000/01-2016/12 (Source: Defra, 2017)

According to DEFRA (2020), in 2016, the latest years that authoritative figures are available, the UK produced 222.9 million tonnes of waste of which England was responsible for 85%. As the chart below shows, the majority (61%) is from construction followed by commercial waste (18.7%).

Household waste, which all of us have direct responsibility in creating, at 27.3 million tonnes (estimated to have declined to 26 million tonnes last year), 12.2% in 2016, might seem almost insignificant.

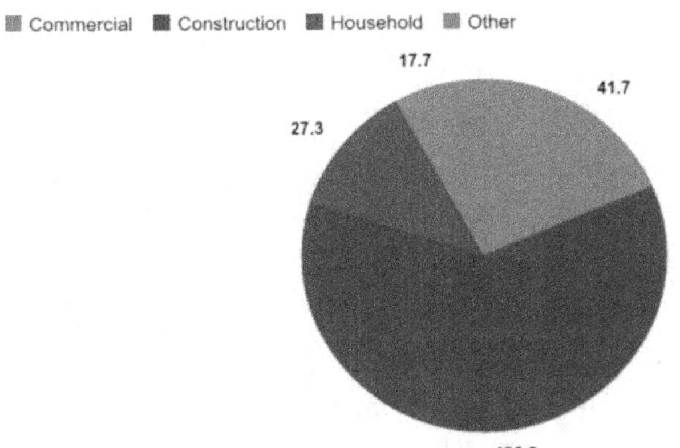

Source: DEFRA (2020)

Waste is, of course, not just a British problem. The World Bank estimate that globally, 2.01 billion tonnes of "municipal solid waste", is produced annually (2021). By the middle of this century, they contend, this figure will increase to 3.4 billion tonnes, double the projected rate of population growth on the next three decades. What is significant, according to the World Bank, is that "high income countries", representing 16% of the global population, produce 683 million tonnes which is just over a third of global waste.

Waste blights the environment. Waste we do not wish to recycle, particularly plastic, because it is cheaper to do so, is sent abroad to developing countries. The problem of waste disproportionately affects the poorest in the world. As critics repeatedly ask, is there not an alternative? Why can't we emulate the 'make do and mend' approach practiced by citizens during the second world war? Why can we not make greater use of existing resources rather than continuing to consume them at the present rate? That is the fundamental doctrine of a circular economy.

Examining Principles of a Circular Economy

Concern about how we collectively make and consume, requiring ever more resources, which in turn increases energy use leading to rising greenhouse gases emissions and results in inevitable waste so harmful to the environment and health, has led to critics calling for what's known as the circular economy. There are according to the Ellen Macarthur Foundation (2021), three key principles: Reduction of waste and pollution through better design; Longer lifespan of everything we use, including all components, through reuse and repair; Greater attention to sustenance of natural systems.

Underpinning improvement are two vital changes. Firstly, the critical imperative we use fewer resources through greater re-use and recycling, should logically result in significantly reduced use of energy that's proven so harmful to the environment. Secondly, correspondingly, any energy requirements should be achieved through utilisation of renewable (green) forms of power. Developing such an approach to our system of production and consumption by every business, government and individual, is explicitly intended of to reduce the vicious circle which currently exists. Instead, a virtuous cycle is possible:

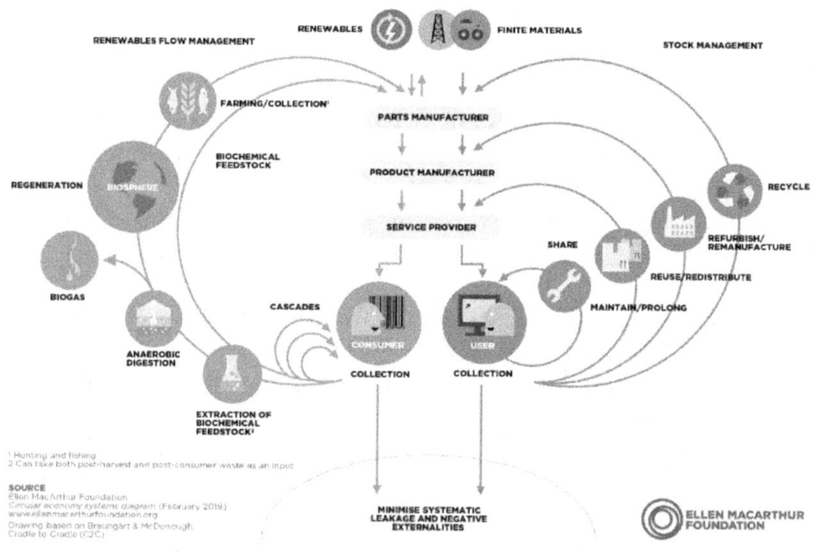

Clearly, given the magnitude of the problem confronting every society, especially those most affluent, there is much to be gained through a change in the approach to what is described by the Ellen Macarthur Foundation as the "take-make-waste extractive industrial model". This requires all of us to engage in a radical culture shift. Individual action becomes collectively significant and marginal gains will ensure aggregate improvement. As the Ellen Macarthur Foundation state on their website (https://www.ellenmacarthurfoundation.org/circular-economy/concept) we all benefit as:

> "Transitioning to a circular economy does not only amount to adjustments aimed at reducing the negative impacts of the linear economy. Rather, it represents a systemic shift that builds long-term resilience, generates business and economic opportunities, and provides environmental and societal benefits."

Radical Change is Possible – But How?

Development of society requires food and shelter. History is replete with advances in technology creating the basis of the environment enjoyed by all advanced economies such as the UK. Progress, measured in economic growth (gross domestic product) and wealth, requires even greater exploitation of the earth's resources. Traditionally, it's believed that reduction in use of such resources will prove detrimental to societal advancement. However, as noted at the outset of this chapter, use of resources at current levels is already having a devastating impact on the globe. Unless we reduce our dependency on the earth's resources, we will destroy the planet for future generations. Accordingly, it's axiomatic we collectively eschew the 'take, make and dispose' approach of the 'linear economy' and replace it with 'make, use and recycle'. Circularity of the economy thus becomes attainable.

A CIRCULAR ECONOMY AIMS TO DECOUPLE VALUE CREATION FROM THE USE OF LIMITED RESOURCES

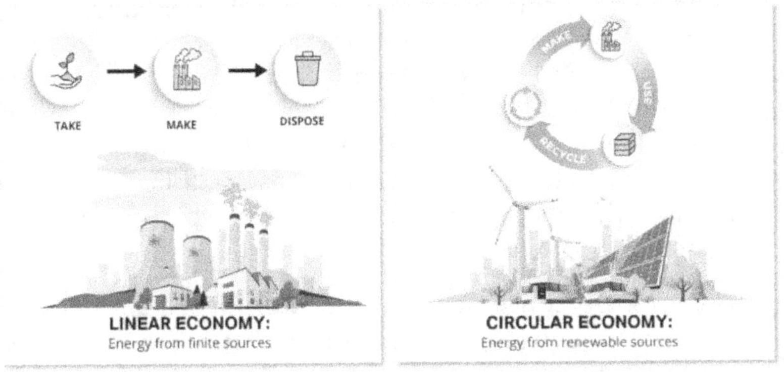

Source: LANXESS website (2021)

Creating a circular economy will produce environmental and health benefits for all parts of the world, most particularly amongst the world's poorest citizens. Avoiding the impending catastrophe will need a conscious shift in everyone's behaviour. Only through cultural change involving every individual will it be possible to achieve the transformation that leads to economies in which carbon neutrality becomes the norm.

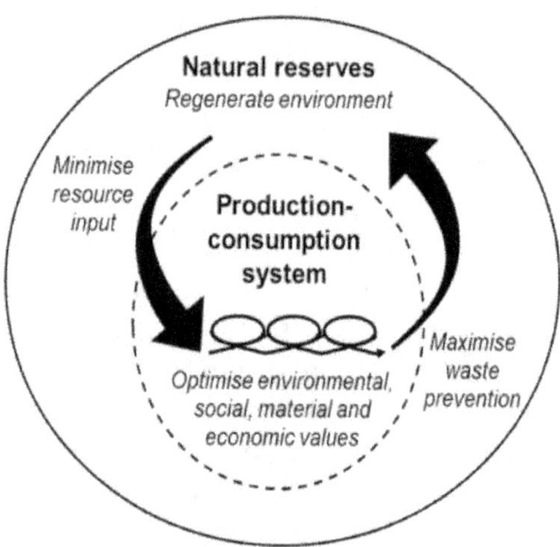

Source: Velenturf and Purnel (2020)

In creating greater circularity, it's useful to distinguish between technical and biological cycles.

Technical cycles are those ones in which the design of every aspect of what we consume is considered and sustainably enhanced. Cursory examination of everything we buy reveals over-elaborate packing, including carboard and plastic, intended to protect items in transit. Packaging should be designed to reduce waste. Many items are designed with very limited use before failure and obsolescence. Redesign should produce items in which use is longer, repair more economic and, where necessary, materials and components can be easily recycled.

Biological cycles are concerned with the way in which materials are created through biological processes. Ideally, after use, they should be capable of being returned to their natural state by composting or anaerobic digestion. Food could be designed to ensure any waste can create energy or used to regenerate living systems intended to create food in the future. For example, in Singapore airline food waste is converted into insect protein meal (Byrne, 2021). This equally applies to, for instance, timber which will eventually rot away and contribute to growth elsewhere.

Anne Velenturf, Research Impact Fellow in Circular Economy and Phil Purnell, Professor of Materials and Structures, University of Leeds, in *The Conversation,* examine what a sustainable circular economy consists of (2020). As they assert, it's estimated that "99%" of what we buy is discarded within six months of purchasing. Velenturf and Purnell stress the importance of three objectives in successful implementation of a circular economy: Closing loops with energy from waste; Increased recycling; Greater sustainability.

Reducing burning of waste, though producing electricity, and greater recycling is crucial they argue. However, they acknowledge, recycling depends on the material. As the diagram below clearly demonstrates, over the last nine years, though there's been some improvement in most material recycling, metal being most notable, the rates are not terribly impressive:

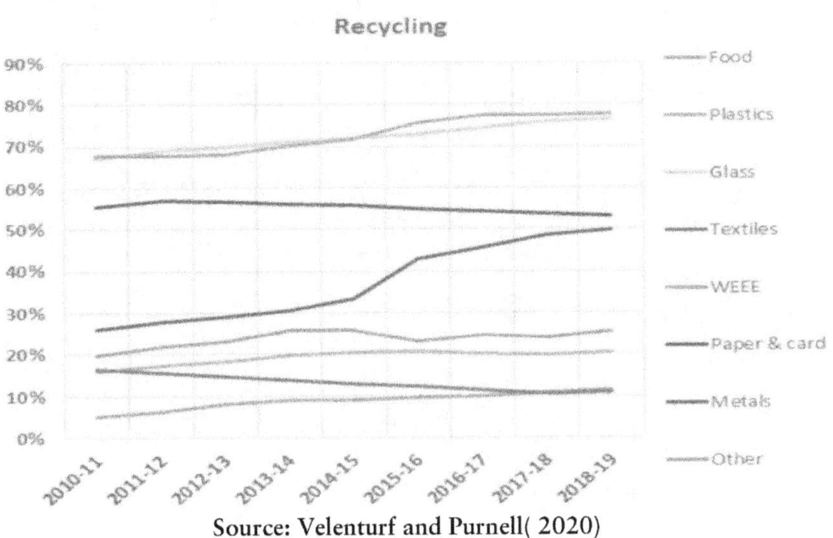

Source: Velenturf and Purnell(2020)

Textiles, especially clothing, is a particular issue of concern. Given our propensity to buy clothes, on average a UK citizen purchases 26.7kg each year (the highest in Europe), the fact a very large proportion is quickly discarded and incinerated rather than being recycled, reduced to 11% in 2019 from 17% in 2010, represents a lost opportunity. Velenturf and Purnell stress the absolute importance of ensuring textiles, as with all other products, are made of materials produced in a sustainable way and including as large a proportion as possible that's recycled. Though considered difficult, they point out that without action, even addressing plastic packaging recycling targets, "more than 50 new recycling plants would be needed in England."

In creating greater sustainability, the third of Velenturf and Purnell's objectives, there are "opportunities" for new models of working to emerge. In seeking alternatives to the linear economy, they suggest, we'll embrace new ways of thinking about what's important. For instance, we will be more inclined to lease clothes rather than buying and disposing (Nazir, 2020). Additionally, there's likely to be production of bespoke items people actually want and place greater value on, than mass consumption of things we don't really need. There is a good argument that the impetus of urgent change will be the catalysts for innovation and creativity.

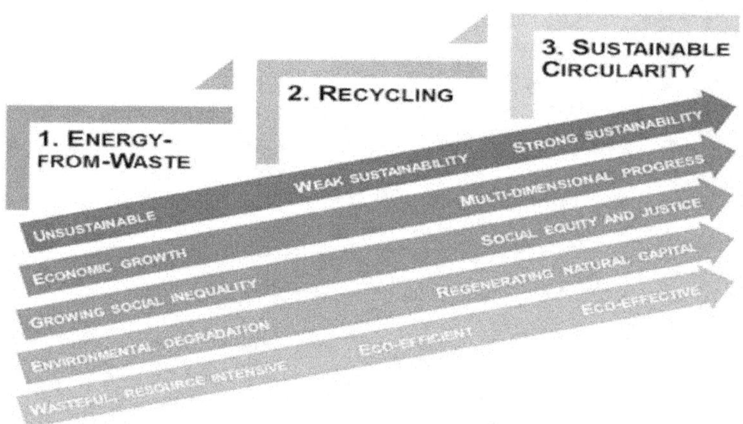

Source: Velenturf and Purnell (2020)

Conclusion – will it work?

Critically, moving to a circular economy will create new jobs. Velenturf and Purnell contend that four times as many jobs are possible based on reuse, leasing, repair and remanufacturing than in waste treatment, disposal and recycling. This, they believe, offers the potential to "generate local economic activity, helping to strengthen relations within communities." A recent report by Green New Deal UK, a non-profit group, asserts that with sufficient stimulus intended to produce the sort of greener economy aligning with the principles of circularity, more than 1.2 million jobs could be created within two years and more than 2.7 million within a decade (Greene, 2021).

In a post-covid age when the economy is recovering following the worst health crisis to affect the world in over a century, there are benign circumstances conducive to producing the radical transformation needed. Any belief we cannot afford the cost of altering to become a circular economy, should be balanced against the fact we can no longer afford the dreadful consequences the current approach to production and consumption entails. The linear model is as inequitable to as many of the world's population as it's destructive to the planet.

References

Byrne, S. (2021), 'Singapore partnership looks to convert airline food waste into insect protein meal', *Feed navigator.com*, https://www.feednavigator.com/Article/2021/05/05/Converting-airline-food-waste-into-insect-protein-meal?utm_source=copyright&utm_medium=OnSite&utm_campaign=copyright accessed 6th May

DEFRA (2017), *Statistics on waste managed by local authorities in England in 2016/17*, Official Statistics, London

DEFRA (2020), *UK Statistics on Waste*, Official Statistics, London

Ellen Macarthur Foundation (2021), *The Circular Economy in Detail*, https://www.ellenmacarthurfoundation.org/explore/the-circular-economy-in-detail, accessed 6th May

Greene, T. (2021), 'Green stimulus plan could create 1.2m UK jobs in two years, research finds', *Guardian*, 20th April, https://www.theguardian.com/environment/2021/apr/20/green-stimulus-plan-uk-jobs-green-new-deal accessed 6th May

Intergovernmental Panel on Climate Change (IPCC) (2007), *Fourth Assessment Report, Impacts, Adaptation and Vulnerability*, Cambridge University Press, Cambridge, England

LANXESS (2021), *Circular Economy, Supporting the transformation of the society towards a sustainable, resource efficient and carbon neutral economy*, https://lanxess.com/en/Responsibility/Societal-Added-Value/Circular-Economy, accessed 6th May

Ministry of Information (2007), *Make Do and Mend,* Imperial War Museum, London

Nazir, S. (2020) 'Clothing rental services – a viable option for UK consumers?', *Retail Gazette,* 23rd September, https://www.retailgazette.co.uk/blog/2020/09/clothing-rental-services-fashion-waste-consumers-recycling-uk-retail/ accessed 6th May

Velenturf, A., and Purnell, P. (2020), 'What a sustainable circular economy would look like', *The Conversation, https://theconversation.com/what-a-sustainable-circular-economy-would-look-like-133808,* accessed 6th May

World Bank (2021), *Trends in Solid Waste Management,* https://datatopics.worldbank.org/what-a-waste/trends_in_solid_waste_management.html#:~:text=The%20world%20generates%202.01%20billion,from%200.11%20to%204.54%20kilograms, accessed 6th May

› Chapter Three

Green economic models – what are they and how may they be accelerated?

Vicky Pryce, Economist and Visiting Professor, Birmingham City University

Keywords: circular economy discussion; ecology v economy; biodiversity and green economics; Green entrepreneurship

Overview

Economics has been crucial in bringing the issue of climate change to the attention of politicians and elevating the need to act among the public. World temperatures rising by more than 2% would lead to catastrophic events and huge loss of life. In the UK, the Climate Change Review of 2006 led by the then Government Economics Service's Nick, now Lord, Stern, was asked to develop information on the cost of climate change. He wanted to compare the costs of acting to doing nothing. We are increasingly aware that climate change may have huge repercussions in terms of the environment, health, food production, lost livelihoods. With those advocating action stressing the potential for general disruption to the world order, leading to turbulence in markets, it is clear that this issue should be tackled with urgency.

Stern's analysis suggested potential loss in world GDP (Gross Domestic Product) caused by climate change could range from 5% to 20% each year. He recommended that the world should spend 1% of global GDP per annum (p.a.) to avoid the worst outcome, and 2% of GDP p.a. to ensure temperatures stabilise at an 'acceptable level'. The cost benefit was clear. Start acting immediately, including imposing a carbon tax combined with other environmental taxes to incentivise the reduction of carbon emissions. Stern imputed social cost of carbon was $85 a ton at the time.

To achieve the Climate Change Review, some crucial assumptions about 'Social Time Preference' were made. It's commonly perceived that the general population's, as well as politicians', time preferences are very much on the short-term. Long-term aspirations are, of course, a long way in the future. We tend to 'discount' the future in preference for utility now. In UK public policy, the long-term discount rate for public investment is set at 3.5%. If we invested £100 now and maturity is after 100 years, discounted it would only be worth £5. We tend not to worry about future generations. Radically altered thinking was needed.

Rethinking Economic Models

Stern and his team recognised this. Controversially, the welfare of all generations, current and future, was treated more or less equally. A Social Time Preference Discount Rate of just 0.1%, though an overall discount rate of 1.4%, was employed; much lower than normal for calculating long term-cost and benefit of public policy capital expenditure decisions. Usual rates discount future benefits heavily making the value of earlier spending higher. However, the low discount rate used in the Stern review had the effect of giving investment now almost the same importance as if spent later, even if benefits accrue to subsequent generations. Zenghelis (2014) explains that this did not go uncontested.

As a review by Geoffrey Heal pointed out, it's not easy to find a way to ensure choices made are consistent and efficient, avoid wasting money, but ensure all generations, extant and future, are treated equally. In terms of environmental impact caused by human behaviour leading to climate change, as we're currently experiencing, one approach would be to continually adapt policies and actions to align with emerging evidence or as prevailing circumstances change (Heal, 2007). Some objected to this methodology (Varian, 2006). However, climate change is acknowledged to be a phenomenally important issue. If left un-checked its impact will increase and, as a consequence, become even more expensive later.

Fifteen years on from the Stern Review, where are we now in economic thinking and practice? Though there has been much discussion, the reality is that we agree that there is still no 'technically correct' intergenerational discount rate. It's axiomatic that economic policy making cannot be a 'value-free science'. Moral considerations, though essential, are difficult to ascribe value to. As a result, the discount rate has been, as usual, a compromise. The UK Government's Green Book, providing guidance on how cost benefit analysis should be carried out for public sector spending, is more explicit. It's accepted that long-term projects can involve substantial intergenerational transfers. It has also concluded that such projects should continue to use the standard discount rate of 3.5% for the first 30 years but thereafter supplemented with a lower and declining discount rate allowing greater emphasis on the welfare of future generations.

Externalities and Biodiversity

In addition to any moral imperatives, there's still an economic imperative to properly price-in externalities in whatever we do and, where necessary, intervene to correct market failure. This applies not just to issues of climate change, but also to environmental degradation more generally. Intervention, as Professor Dasgupta's Review on the Economics of Biodiversity makes clear (2021), is that externalities in relation to environmental degradation are not captured by the standard measures of GDP which ignore the nature and depreciation of natural assets. Finance has to adjust to these longer-term risks and incorporate nature to a much greater extent in decision systems (Dasgupta, *ibid*). Interestingly the Bank of England has now been instructed by the Chancellor of the Exchequer to incorporate climate change risks into Monetary Policy decisions.

What is clear is that action is urgently required. Despite an estimated 7% fall in carbon emissions during 2020 due to the pandemic, this is now being reversed and the stock of CO_2 remains high and will inevitably rise again as economies recover. The latest UNEP report (Haustfather, 2020), asserts that current commitments under the Paris agreement by individual countries through nationally determined contributions (NDCs), will result only in a levelling-off of carbon emissions rather than a decline. This would not meet the goals set by the agreement which aimed to ensure temperature rise to a maximum of 1.5C above pre-industrial levels (see Climate Action Tracker Website, 2021).

Nevertheless, as Climate Action Tracker point out, some progress has been identified. New net zero ambitions have resulted in new measures being announced and markets are acknowledging that and pricing the risk it into share price expectations. Finance is gradually shifting away from polluting companies and sectors. Data from the US suggests that as at the end of 2020 sustainable investing, mindful of ESG (Environmental, Social and Governance) issues in their selection criteria, accounted for approximately 33% of all funds under management (Nason, 2020). President Biden's statements to abide by

Paris commitments, in direct contrast to his predecessor, provides a significant boost to this trend. The EU's pledge to achieve climate-neutrality by 2050 through ambitious investment raised by green bonds as part of its Euro750b Recovery and Sustainability Plan is equally demonstrative of positive intervention. Even China, still investing in new coal fired power stations and now twice as large a polluter as the US, has unveiled its intention to achieve net zero by 2060. Governments across the globe are aware of the criticality of the need for change in behaviour by citizens and companies and are edging it along.

The UK Experience

In the UK, pressure to tackle climate change and reshape thinking post-pandemic, has led to increased emphasis by investors on ESG credentials of firms into which funds are directed. With the UK hosting the COP26 international climate change conference in Glasgow in November there are attempts to position the country as a leader in the fight against climate change. It might be expected therefore that this would provide impetus to redress the fact that the yield from environmental taxes in the UK has been declining. In 1997, government receipts from such taxes amounted to 8.4% but by 2019, this figure was just 7%. Yet, recent budgets have done little so far to support the green agenda.

Fuel duty has remained unchanged for 10 years and there are concerns that the switch to a new UK Emissions Trading Scheme, having just left the EU, may not provide by itself the impetus required. There is also the anomaly that the UK continues to subsidise gas-fired heating at an effective rate of £14 per tonne of carbon. The government has also scrapped the £1.5 billion green homes deal grant subsidising insulation or low-carbon heating (Harvey, 2021) as well as cutting subsidies for electric vehicle purchases. And yet it is estimated that households worldwide emit some 72% of all greenhouse gases. Homes emit 14% of CO_2 in the UK. Clearly incentives should address the need to encourage households to use less energy.

In their defence, ministers point to the considerable subsidies given to renewables, particularly wind, over the years and also, more recently, the announcement of a £12 billion 'initial fund' for climate change investments with a 10-point plan for change. Although the government expects this sum to be supplemented by private sector finance, the Climate Change Committee calculates that the figure for overall investment should be a much larger £50b per annum between now and 2030.

Some of that extra investment may indeed materialise. But would a series of targeted incentives explicitly intended to shift collective behaviour also assist? Behavioural economists assert that in terms of climate change policy, normal monetary incentives do not work in isolation (Gowdy, 2008). For some, lower household bills could be inducement to change behaviour. However, to achieve change at the scale required, there needs to be widespread education and explanation providing evidence of the scale of the threat posed by climate change to ensure the motivation for action is there. And this would need to be supplemented by outlining additionally the potential benefits that will accrue to everyone from social health and general well-being from changed energy use in our homes (Stankuniene et al, 2020). This is important as altering household behaviour could lead to 6-16% cut in greenhouse gas emissions (Van De Ven *et al*, 2018).

The Circular Economy

Advocates of the circular economy argue that energy saving is also possible through households being engaged in increasing recycling of waste produced (Ellen MacArthur Foundation, 2019). And more can be achieved by applying those principles also at the industry level. The UN supported definition of a circular economy is one that is a *"regenerative system in which resource input and waste, emission, and energy leakage are minimized by slowing, closing, and narrowing energy and material loops"* (United Nations, 2019. As the UN points out, only *9% of the "92.8 billion tonnes of minerals, fossil fuels, metals and biomass"* used in the world each year is recycled.

The evidence of the waste in the economy is stark: 90% of the materials used in manufacturing in Europe becomes waste before leaving the factory. We throw away 80% of products made in Europe within the first six months of production (Judge Business School, 2021). Much can be done if one were focussing on encouraging better design of goods which last and which therefore ease the process of maintenance and repair, allow their re-use, refurbishment and, ultimately, their recycling (*ibid*).

Indeed, there are aspects of the circular economy in the UK's first ever industrial decarbonisation strategy published in March 2021 (McDonald, 2021). Re-manufacturing and recycling, thereby improving energy efficiency, is part of the what the newly established Infrastructure Bank is meant to achieve through a mixture of incentives and direct support. Creating new sources of greener energy and promotion of energy saving innovation in industrial processes is vital. Increased use of digital technology, investment in low-carbon hydrogen (green rather than blue), and in carbon capture and storage, talked about but never properly supported, are some of the areas where serious progress needs to be made. But doing it in such a way that truly engages the private sector, and for the longer term, is crucial.

Looking ahead

There is reason to be cautiously optimistic. Some earlier policies have assisted. Direct subsidisation of alternative fuels has altered market fundamentals. Many renewables are now cheaper to produce than fossil fuels. There's progress in 'greening' electricity though much more needs to be achieved in transport and in improving energy efficiency in homes. Regulatory changes will soon make combustion engines in cars obsolete. Much is suggested about the opportunities of the 'new' green economy to propel growth and create new jobs.

Innovation, creativity and imagination will be key. There has in fact been some evidence already that the emergence of 'green entrepreneurship' is contributing to new, innovative thinking in this area (IED, 2020). But much more will be needed. Dimitri Zenghelis, a leading climate change economist and Senior Visiting Fellow at the Grantham Research Institute at the LSE, emphasises how decisions taken now will affect the potential for transformation to take place, so timing is of the essence. But it will be important not to think in a static way and try and shape the future on the basis of current technology. Instead, one should engage in such a way, partnering between state and private sector, that allows for the needed technology transformation to materialise. Indeed, rather than assuming that the transition will be costly and permanently reduce GDP, we can turn it around and in fact benefit in the long-term from what may well be sustainably lower energy costs as we transit from a carbon-based infrastructure, we have inherited to renewables that do exactly what it 'says on the tin', they renew themselves instead of becoming exhausted and more costly in the process.

About the Author

Economist: Vicky Pryce is Chief Economic Adviser and a board member at the Centre for Economics and Business Research (CEBR) and Visiting Professor at Birmingham City University. She was previously Senior Managing Director at FTI Consulting, Director General for Economics at the Department for Business, Innovation and Skills (BIS) and Joint Head of the UK Government Economic Service. She was a Partner at the accounting and consulting firm KPMG after senior economic positions in banking and the oil sector. She sits on the Council of the Institute for Fiscal Studies and on the Economic Advisory Group of the British Chambers of Commerce.

References

Climate Action Tracker Website (2021), 'Paris temperature goal, Conceptualising the Paris Agreement long-term temperature goal', https://climateactiontracker.org/methodology/paris-temperature-goal/ accessed 8th May

Dasgupta, P. (2021), *The Economics of Biodiversity: The Dasgupta Review*, HM Treasury, London

Ellen MacArthur Foundation, (2019), *Completing the Picture: How the Circular Economy Tackles Climate*, https://www.ellenmacarthurfoundation.org/assets/downloads/Completing_The_Picture_How_The_Circular_Economy-_Tackles_Climate_Change_V3_26_September.pdf, accessed 8th May

Gowdy, J. M. (2008), 'Behavioral Economics and Climate Change Policy', *Journal of Economic Behavior & Organization*, vol 68 (3-4), pp. 632-644, December

Haustfather, Z. (2020), 'UNEP: Net-zero pledges provide an 'opening' to close growing emissions 'gap'', Carbon Brief, 9th December, https://www.carbonbrief.org/unep-net-zero-pledges-provide-an-opening-to-close-growing-emissions-gap, accessed 8th May

Harvey, F. (2021), 'UK government scraps green homes grant after six months', Guardian, 27th March, https://www.theguardian.com/environment/2021/mar/27/uk-government-scraps-green-homes-grant-after-six-months, accessed 8th May

Heal, G. (2007), 'Discounting: A Review of the Basic Economics', *The University of Chicago Law Review*, vol. 74, pp. 59-77

IED (2020), 'Green Entrepreneurship. Sustainable development for business', Institute of Entrepreneurship Development, 15th July, https://ied.eu/blog/green-entrepreneurship-sustainable-development-for-business/, **accessed 8th May**

Judge Business School (2021), *Circular Economy and Sustainability Strategies,* University of Cambridge https://online.em.jbs.cam.ac.uk/circular-economy-sustainability-strategies?utm_source=Google&utm_medium=c&utm_term=%2Bcircular%20%2Beconomy&utm_location=9045894&utm_campaign=B-365D_UK_GG_SE_CCES_Core&utm_content=Circular-Economy_BBT&gclid=EAIaIQobChMIq8bAjfXS7wIVCdTtCh2I8QRSEAAYASAAEgISkfD_BwE, accessed 8th May

McDonald, N. (2021), 'World first' industrial decarbonisation strategy developed in the UK', *Pinsent Masons Website*, 19th March, https://www.pinsentmasons.com/out-law/news/world-first-industrial-decarbonisation-strategy-developed-uk, accessed 8th May

Nason, D. (2020), "Sustainable investing' is surging, accounting for 33% of total U.S. assets under management', *CNBC*, 21st December, https://www.cnbc.com/2020/12/21/sustainable-investing-accounts-for-33percent-of-total-us-assets-under-management.html, accessed 8th May

Roberts, D. (2012), 'Discount rates: A boring thing you should know about (with otters!)', *Grist*, 24th September, https://grist.org/article/discount-rates-a-boring-thing-you-should-know-about-with-otters/, accessed 7th May

Stankuniene, G., Streimikiene, D. and Kyriakopoulos, G.L. (2020), Systematic Literature Review on Behavioral Barriers of Climate Change Mitigation in Households, *Sustainability*, vol 12 (18), pp.1-18

United Nations (2019), 'Circular Economy Crucial for Paris Climate Goals', *UN Climate Change News,* 22nd January, https://unfccc.int/news/circular-economy-crucial-for-paris-climate-goals, accessed 8th May

Varian, H. (2006), 'Recalculating the Costs of Global Climate Change', *The New York Times*, 14th December, https://www.nytimes.com/2006/12/14/business/14scene.html, accessed 7th May

Van De Ven, D., Gonzalez-Eguino, M. and Arto, I. (2018), The potential of behavioural change for climate change mitigation: a case study for the European Union, *Mitigation and Adaptation Strategies for Global Change*, vol. 23(6), pp. 853-886, August.

Zenghelis, D. (2014), 'A flawed conversation about the Stern Review', *Grantham Research Institute on Climate Change and the Environment,* London School of Economics and Political Science, 3rd April, https://www.lse.ac.uk/granthaminstitute/news/a-flawed-conversation-about-the-stern-review/, accessed 7th May

Chapter Four

It's a sustainable economy, or it's no economy

Tony Juniper, Chair, Nature Conservation Agency and Fellow, the University of Cambridge Institute for Sustainability Leadership

Overview

Stark scientific reports charting the decline of Nature and shifts in the Earth's climate system have been in circulation for more than three decades. From the Brundtland World Commission on Environment and Development in 1987 (Brundtland Commission, 1987), to the scientists warning (see Union of Concerned Scientists, (1992), issued to the 1992 Earth Summit and from the successive reports from the Intergovernmental Panel on Climate Change[1] to periodic Global Biodiversity Assessments[2], there have been numerous warnings as to the scale of peril faced by human societies arising from unsustainable patterns of development.

For a long period, the reaction to these warnings was at worst dismissive and often at best seen in the adoption of modest sectoral environmental policies. These related to, for example, energy efficiency, the creation of protected areas, recycling targets, reducing the most toxic water and air pollution and moves toward less damaging management of natural resources, such as fish and forests. Often worthwhile and positive in their own narrow terms, these environmental policies have made matters less bad, but largely failed to appreciably reduce the overall scale of human demand, nor the overall impact of that on the health of the Biosphere (Juniper, 2016).

---

[1] The Intergovernmental Panel on Climate Change conducts periodic cycles of research into climate change. The IPCC's Sixth Assessment Report will be published in 2021. https://www.ipcc.ch/reports/

[2] The Convention on Biological Diversity conducts periodic cycles into the status of biodiversity. The fifth outlook report was published in 2020. https://www.cbd.int/gbo/

It's the economy, stupid

The fact that most of the key indicators, from deforestation (Shulte et al 2019), to greenhouse gas emissions (Richie and Rosser, 2017) and from threatened species (IPBES, 2019) to soil loss (Richie and Rosser, 2017), have not only remained unsustainable, but worsened, confirms the inadequacy of the response to date, and begs what is perhaps the most important question of all – namely, why after all the warnings and new policies are things still heading in the wrong direction?

The simple answer to that relates to the fact that while environmental policies have evolved and sometimes improved markedly, the fundamentals of the human relationship with the natural systems that sustain people and the rest of life have barely altered. That relationship is mediated in large part by our economic system, and the manner in which at almost every turn our economy has deepened the mismatch between human demand and what natural systems can sustainably supply (Juniper, 2013).

What to do about this has proven a difficult question to debate, not least because the health of Nature and the health of the economy have often been seen as mutually exclusive subjects, with the protection of the former being widely seen as a threat to the latter.

The tension has been repeatedly evidenced in commentary and narrative, including when even modest environmental policy has been attacked for being a brake on economic growth, undermining competitiveness, putting up consumer prices or leading to job losses[1]. The fact that there has been scant evidence to support any of that (often quite to the contrary with environmental regulation shown to be a driver of innovation in business models and technology (International Chemical Secretariat, 2004), this 'economy first' view has been a major reason why progress toward sustainable outcomes has as yet been too elusive.

Sceptical voices that first attacked the science later moved to an economic narrative, claiming that even if climate change and a mass extinction event were under way, it made more sense to continue with

---

[1] British Chancellor of the Exchequer George Osborne during his time in office on several occasions made attacks on environmental policies as a result of their claimed impact on businesses and jobs. For example, see https://www.bbc.co.uk/news/uk-politics-17479165

economic growth as the primary overriding priority (Lomborg, 2001). That view has been reflected by various think tanks and commentators and featured on the platforms of prominent Heads of State, such as President Bolsonaro of Brazil and US President Donald Trump.

The changing narrative

The environment versus economy debate has, however, not been static and during recent years there have been a slew of expert processes, reports and initiatives that have made it abundantly clear how a failure to halt and reverse ecological degradation will in the end lead to crippling economic and security costs, and at a far greater scale than is entailed with dealing with these challenges up front.

For example, Millennium Ecosystem Assessment (2005), highlighted how environmental decline would undermine prospects for meeting social goals. The following year saw the publication of the Stern Review (2006), which highlighted how proactively addressing climate change through low carbon development would be far cheaper than dealing with the consequences. In 2010 The Economics of Ecosystems and Biodiversity (Sukhdev et al, 2010), set out the vast value of Nature for the economy, highlighting how healthy natural systems were, among other things, 'the GDP of the poor'. The seminal research from Robert Costanza and his colleagues (2014) revealed how the annual economic value of Nature's services far exceed global GDP. Recently, the Dasgupta Review (2021), commissioned by the UK Treasury, marked the latest learned assessment to underline the interdependence between ecology and economy, highlighting how these two fundamental system elements must be joined, not separated or seen as mutually exclusive priorities.

All of this and more leads to a simple message, that is, if we are to protect and sustain human welfare, achieve lasting poverty reduction and security, then economic development needs to lead to the *regeneration* of ecological systems, not their progressive continuing degradation. This requires something of a shift in mind-set, based on a new realisation in economics that Nature not only as a set of 'natural resources' to be consumed, or at best sustainably managed through environmental policy, but a provider of essential services, including carbon capture, freshwater replenishment, nutrient recycling, a source of resilience to climate change, essential for health and wellbeing, an inspiration for design and the genetic library that underpins all of our food and much of our medicine.

Those values are presently largely invisible in economics, leading to the liquidation of system assets, while counting those losses as 'growth'.

This reality raises a further vital question.

What is the economy for?

For many decades, and especially since the period following the Second World War, economics has been geared to the central goal of expanding GDP. This overriding and pervasive goal has coloured the policy mix of countries worldwide, and as was pointed out above, sometimes fostered a sceptical approach toward ambitious environmental goals. GDP essentially measures the throughput of transactions in the economy via the sum value of services and products sold and has historically proven to be a broad proxy for the volume of energy and resources being consumed although some countries, such as the UK, have during recent times for example begun to delink GDP growth from greenhouse gas emissions (see Agbugba *et al*, 2019).

While the size of GDP has been subject to forensic tracking and shown to be broadly increasing, our understanding of the countervailing and related loss of function in natural systems has not been measured to anything like the same extent (despite all the reports), nor influenced economics in ways that we can now see it must urgently do. As GDP has gone up, usually in line with resource depletion and the release of pollution, we have been growing the part of the economy we measure, but failing to measure the progressive destruction of that part of the economy that we don't (Nature), but which has been shown to be bigger and more valuable that the part we do measure.

The obsession with GDP growth has become so pervasive and single minded that its pursuit has in many countries become an end in itself. This is based on assumptions as to how the consequences will be broadly positive, with more jobs, reduced poverty, larger tax receipts and improved food and energy security following in its wake. If, however, all of this is achieved through the degradation of the Biosphere, then economics in its present form is a doomed project, and one that must change and adapt to the situation before it. To do this, it is necessary to be clear about what the economy and economics is for.

Considering what we know, it is clear that we need to look more broadly than increasing GDP, and the undoubted (but inevitably limited) benefits that it can provide. That new economic idea might be expressed in terms of providing for comfortable and rewarding lives for the 10 billion people expected to be on Earth in the second half of this century, while sustaining and restoring the health of the biosphere. There are many elements to this, and many tools that might be employed, but the shape of that new economic vehicle can already be glimpsed, as new approaches take hold and new agendas emerge.

A new economic vehicle

One way to envisage the transformation required is to literally consider the economy as a vehicle, and one that will take humankind to that new destination, where comfort and fulfilling lives can be secured for everyone within planetary capacities.

Under the bonnet of that vehicle is a purring engine. It is made from private sector companies, they are the driving force of the economy, calibrated and honed by science and technology, they innovate to create products and services that protect and restore the Biosphere. In the driving seat is Government, it has its eye on data and driven by policy and law, as it steers the vehicle toward the ultimate destination, changing direction where needed by keeping a close eye on the road ahead. Into the fuel tank goes green fuel, in the form of trillions of dollars of finance from private investment, pension funds and other savings. That fuel seeks sustainable returns, powering the engine by backing zero carbon, Nature-positive and circular economy outcomes. On the dashboard is the SatNav. Programmed by the voters and consumers who are the ultimate beneficiaries of heading toward the destination, and who increasingly wish to see progress to a sustainable outcome.

Some companies and financial institutions are now adopting strategies to do this, while some Governments are getting behind the wheel in that new economic vehicle, where from the driving seat they can reach buttons and controls, including regulations, tax regimes, trade policy and spending choices, all of which can drive the car in the right direction. One articulation of what the destination will be like has been captured in the notion of donut economics (Raworth, 2018), whereby human wellbeing and social goals are pursued and met within planetary boundaries.

On the speedometer is a new measure to replace GDP. It still measures growth, but not only the throughput of consumption in products and services, but also the extent to which people are enjoying secure, long and happy lives, within the ecological boundaries of our finite world.

The need to augment GDP with measures of planetary health are now becoming more mainstream, with for example the 2021 Dasgupta Review highlighting the need for measure of 'inclusive wealth' and the United Nations adopting a new framework to measure the contribution of Nature to economic wellbeing (UN, 2021).

Planetary boundaries

The economy is a human construct, whereas ecology is a finite system. The result is that on one side there is the assumption in economic models that growth in GDP can theoretically be infinite (and in many models is treated as such), and on the other are the limits to growth, which although known about for decades, have in economics been largely ignored. The longer this clash of realities goes on, the more serious will be the risks to human wellbeing, and our economy.

As the climate system shifts toward a new state and as the loss of ecosystem function and mass extinction of species continue to gather pace, our choices are ever more urgent and stark. Continue as we are and expect massive economic costs as ecological decline feeds back into the economic systems, or change the system quickly.

As economic planners and political strategists ponder the options, they might wish to reflect on the impact of our most recent collective experience of what happens when our relationships with the natural world gets out of step with Nature. Following the jump of a coronavirus from bats to humans, likely via an intermediate host such as pangolins, a global disease pandemic has caused economic damage estimated to have a mid-range cost of over 26 trillion dollars (Judge Business School (2021). Pandemic disease is but one of the economically significant risks that is increasing as humans degrade the Biosphere (Juniper, 2020) and in the wake of recent events we have perhaps what is the ultimate warning, with COVID-19 having the potential to achieve what earlier scientific warnings did not, and to put us on new and sustainable path to the future.

About the author

Tony Juniper CBE is Chair of the official Nature conservation agency Natural England and a Fellow with the University of Cambridge Institute for Sustainability Leadership. He is a former Director of Friends of the Earth, Executive Director with WWF UK, President of the Royal Society of Wildlife Trusts, President of the Society for the Environment and environment advisor to HRH the Prince of Wales. He has also advised many international companies and is the author of a number of books, including the best-selling *What has Nature ever done for us?*

References

Agbugba. G., Okoye, G., Giva, M. Marlow, J. (2019), *The decoupling of economic growth from carbon emissions: UK evidence*, Office for National Statistics, London, 21st October,
https://www.ons.gov.uk/economy/nationalaccounts/uksectoraccounts/compendium/economicreview/october2019/thedecouplingofeconomicgrowthfromcarbonemissionsukevidence, accessed 12th May

Brundtland Commission, (1987), Our Common Future, Report of the World Commission on Environment and Development, Oxford University Press, http://www.un-documents.net/our-common-future.pdf, accessed 12th May

Convention on Biological Diversity (2020), Global Biodiversity Outlook, fifth edition, https://www.cbd.int/gbo/, accessed 12th May

Costanza, R., de Groot, R., Sutton, P., Van der Ploeg, S., Anderson, S., Kubiszewski, I., Farber, S. and Kerry Turner, R. (2014), 'Changes in the global value of ecosystem services', *Global Environmental Change*, May, vol 26(1), pp. 152–158
https://www.researchgate.net/publication/262489570_Changes_in_the_global_value_of_ecosystem_services accessed 12th May

Dasgupta, P. (2021), *The Economics of Biodiversity: The Dasgupta Review*, HM Treasury, London.

International Chemical Secretariat (2004), Cry wolf - predicted costs by industry in the face of new regulations, International Chemical Secretariat, April, https://issuu.com/chemsec/docs/cry_wolf_report

IPBES (2019), Summary for policymakers of the global assessment report on biodiversity and ecosystem services of the Intergovernmental Science-Policy Platform on Biodiversity and Ecosystem Services, IPBES secretariat, Bonn, Germany, https://ipbes.net/global-assessment

Judge Business School (2021), 'Economic Impact, The GDP@Risk over five years from COVID-19 could range from $3.3 trillion to $82 trillion, says the Centre for Risk Studies', Centre for Risk Studies, University of Cambridge, 19th May, https://www.jbs.cam.ac.uk/insight/2020/economic-impact/, accessed 12th May

Juniper, T. (2016), What's Really Happening To Our Planet, Dorling Kindersley, London

Juniper, T. (2013), What has Nature ever done for us? Profile Books, London

Juniper, T. (2020), 'This pandemic is an environmental issue', Evening Standard, 7th May, https://www.standard.co.uk/comment/comment/this-pandemic-is-an-environmental-issue-a4434651.html, accessed 12th May

Lomborg, B. (2001), The Skeptical Environmentalist, Cambridge University Press, Cambridge

Millennium Ecosystem Assessment (2005), Ecosystems and Human Wellbeing, General Synthesis, Island Press, https://www.millenniumassessment.org/en/Synthesis.html, accessed 12th May

Panagos, P., Borrelli, P. and Robinson, D. (2020), 'FAO calls for actions to reduce global soil erosion', Mitigation and Adaptation Strategies for Global Change, volume 25, pp. 789–790, https://link.springer.com/content/pdf/10.1007/s11027-019-09892-3.pdf, accessed 12th May

Raworth, K. (2018), Seven ways to think like a 21st century economist, Random House, London

Richie, H. and Rosser, M. (2017), 'CO_2 and Greenhouse Gas Emissions', Our World in Data, https://ourworldindata.org/co2-and-other-greenhouse-gas-emissions, accessed 12th May

Schulte, I. (Coordinating Author), Streck, C. and Roe, S. (2019), Protecting and Restoring Forests: A Story of Large Commitments yet Limited Progress, Five Year Assessment Report, forestdeclaration.org, September, https://forestdeclaration.org/images/uploads/resource/2019NYDFReport.pdf, accessed 12th May

Stern, N. (2006), The Economics of Climate Change: The Stern Review, Cambridge University Press, Cambridge, https://www.lse.ac.uk/GranthamInstitute/publication/the-economics-of-climate-change-the-stern-review/ accessed 12th May

Sukhdev, P., Wittmer, H., Schröter-Schlaack, C., Nesshöver, C., Bishop, J., ten Brink, P., Gundimeda, H., Kumar, P. and Simmons, B. (2010),

Mainstreaming the Economics of Nature: A Synthesis of the Approach, Conclusions and Recommendations of TEEB, The Economics of Ecosystems and Biodiversity, http://teebweb.org/publications/teeb-for/synthesis/, accessed 12th May

Union of Concerned Scientists, (1992), World Scientists' Warning to Humanity, UCS, Washington DC, https://www.ucsusa.org/sites/default/files/attach/2017/11/World%20Scientists%27%20Warning%20to%20Humanity%201992.pdf, accessed 12th May

UN (2021), UN adopts landmark framework to integrate natural capital in economic reporting, United Nations Department of Economic and Social Affairs, https://www.un.org/en/desa/un-adopts-landmark-framework-integrate-natural-capital-economic-reporting, accessed 12th May

Union of Concerned Scientists, (1992), World Scientists' Warning to Humanity, UCS, Washington DC, https://www.ucsusa.org/sites/default/files/attach/2017/11/World%20Scientists%27%20Warning%20to%20Humanity%201992.pdf

Chapter Five

No green economy can thrive without re-writing capitalism's rule book

Jonathon Porritt, Environmental Campaigner

Overview

Much of the advocacy around the idea of a 'Green Economy' suffers from a lot of ideological naivety. Under today's dominant variants of capitalism (in the West and in China), there is very limited scope for any green economy to make much of a difference.

Introduction

I know I shouldn't be so churlish, but if there's one thing that really gets up my nose, it's Larry Fink's annual Letter to Shareholders. As CEO of BlackRock (the world's largest investment managers, with around \$9tn of assets under management), he delivers his latest prognostications for investors (emphasising the importance of addressing climate change) with a degree of self-satisfied authority that they obviously love, sycophantically lapping it all up year after year. This from a man whose company still has holdings of nearly \$85bn in coal companies, having crafted a smart little loophole for his investment managers which means they're still allowed to hold shares in companies that earn less than a quarter of their revenues from coal. The hypocrisy is staggering.

The 2021 Letter concludes with an analysis of why ESG (Environmental, Social, Governance) issues are now more material for investors than ever, highlighting that there was a 96 per cent increase in ESG investing since the year before. From which some might conclude that the idea of a Green Economy has landed even in one of the most powerful bastions of planet-wrecking neoliberal capitalism. So can we all now relax?

Shortly after this year's Letter, the former Chief Investment Officer of Sustainable Investing at BlackRock, Tariq Fancy, who 'led the charge to incorporate ESG into our global investments' (in his own words), gave a rather more accurate picture of the current ESG scene, pointing out that portfolio managers are still legally bound – and handsomely incentivised – to do absolutely nothing that compromises profits. As he put it in a forthright statement in USA Today:

> "Imagine the planet is a cancer patient, and climate change is the cancer. Wall Street is prescribing wheatgrass: a well-marketed, profitable idea that has no chance of curing or even slowing down the cancer. In this scenario, wheatgrass is the deadly distraction, misleading the public and denying lifesaving measures like chemotherapy. But like giving false hope to unproven cures in the midst of a pandemic, the consequences of such irresponsibility are all too obvious. And motivation for why the industry continues to greenwash is all too obvious."

What does this tell us?

For ESG investment to be described as a 'deadly distraction' by one of its foremost advocates in the past, is challenging for all those intent on establishing the transformative potential of a Green Economy. Such an economy, as captured in multiple interpretations in this collection of essays, would undoubtedly be a significant improvement on today's 'Brown Economy'. However, it represents but the smallest step in the transition to a genuinely sustainable economy.

I've rarely come across an articulation of the Green Economy that doesn't depend (more or less unquestioningly) on the idea of 'green growth' – based on the assumption that the economy must continue to grow, year on year, for all sorts of ideological and macroeconomic imperatives, just significantly less destructively as a consequence of current externalities (eg billions of tonnes of greenhouse gas emissions) being internalised through stringent regulation or fiscal sticks and carrots.

It's those imperatives which take us straight to the heart of capitalism today. And any articulation of a Green Economy that doesn't simultaneously interrogate the nature of capitalism can never be much more than a (hopefully) entertaining distraction – as perfectly exemplified in Bill Gates's recently published 'How to Avoid a Climate Disaster' (2021). There's not a single paragraph in this celebration of technocratic innovation that suggests capitalism today might have some deeper problems to confront other than swopping out fossil fuels for renewables.

When I wrote *Capitalism as if the World Matters* (Porritt, 2007), I described capitalism as 'The only overarching system capable of achieving any kind of reconciliation between ecological sustainability, on the one hand, and the pursuit of prosperity and personal wellbeing on the other.' Seventeen years on, I stand by that judgement. Given that we've got no more than a decade to start doing what needs to be done to prevent both runaway climate change and ecosystem collapse, arguments about needing to 'get rid of capitalism' (either through radical yet still constitutional political activism, or through revolution) before any viable solutions become available to us, are clearly self-indulgent fantasies. Not least because we now live in a world which includes more than 2,700 billionaires, any of whom could summon up a private army to thwart any such 'will of the people'. (Not that they would need to. It's absolutely not the will of the people that we should 'get rid of capitalism' anyway: the vast majority of people in the rich world would certainly love to see capitalism 'done better', and the vast majority of people in the poor world would have it on pretty much any terms, but those are very different positions from wanting to be rid of it.)

Even 'capitalism done well' seems a very big ask at the moment. It's clear that capitalism as we know it today is struggling to deliver even light green growth. Externalities are <u>not</u> being internalised – or not in any material way. Nine times out of ten, the 'voluntary principle' is still favoured over robust regulation. Trillions of taxpayers' dollars are still flowing into economic activities that systematically undermine the prospects for a sustainable world, through support for fossil fuels and intensive agriculture. This failure to act explains why investors today (in BlackRock and elsewhere) are still giving this inherently unsustainable economy the benefit of the doubt, even as they begin to come to terms with the scale of the 'stranded asset' challenge which is about to overwhelm them.

Which leaves us with this mind-boggling paradox: it's not intentional anti-capitalist movements that will get rid of capitalism, but rather the two dominant variants of capitalism today. By which I mean:

Variant 1: The West's 40-year-old experiment with neoliberal, small-state capitalism, preferencing the operation of so-called 'free markets' over accountable regulation and all social and cultural norms that are seen to act as barriers to that remorseless marketisation of people's lives. The true cost of this profit-maximising experiment is now laid bare in today's converging crises of accelerating climate change, worsening inequality and collapsing ecosystems.

Variant 2: China's collectivist state capitalism. Since 1979, China's GDP has grown by an average of just under 10% per annum. Even now, President Xi Jinping will not allow economic growth to fall below 6.5%, making this police state (run by 90 million members of the Communist Party) one of the worst drivers of ecological collapse and runaway climate change. Profit is not the primary motive here: maintaining the power and wealth of the Communist Party (through a complex network of State-Owned Enterprises) is ultimately all that matters.

Between them, these still dominant ideologies are completely incapable of delivering any kind of meaningful Green Economy, let alone a genuinely sustainable economy. Another decade of these evil twins reigning supreme all but guarantees that we will pass the point of no return in terms of runaway climate change and ecosystem collapse, which in turn all but guarantees the consequential collapse of 'civilisation' as we know it today. I don't want to get too deep into apocalyptic 'doomism', but it honestly is as simple as that.

A Contemporary View of the Existential Crisis

At the end of February 2021, the latest update from the Secretariat of the UN Framework Convention on Climate Change, as part of its preparations for COP26 to be held in Glasgow this year, informed governments that their revised national plans for emission reductions will, between them, reduce emissions by no more than 1 per cent by the end of the decade. Set that against the headline conclusion of the 2018 Special Report from the Intergovernmental Panel on Climate Change, to ensure average temperature increases by no more than 1.5°C by the end of the century, we have to halve emissions of greenhouse gases by 2030.

That's the gap we now face: 1 per cent versus 50 per cent.

By the time you read this, new commitments from the USA, India and (possibly) China may well have narrowed that gap to around 5 per cent. The Conference in Glasgow may see a few 'white rabbits emerging out of the hat', to narrow it even further to, let's say, 10 per cent versus the required 50 per cent. That would be tantamount to complete failure. Yet how many people advising companies today (from within or without) seriously understand the nature of that challenge? To what extent must we now confront the inconvenient reality that today's articulation of 'corporate sustainability' (just like conventional advocacy on behalf of the Green Economy) falls way short of what is now required?

In that regard, I'm still very proud of the work that Forum for the Future has done with dozens of multinationals over the last 25 years. I've seen, first-hand, how companies can embrace change, move fast, massively reduce negative externalities, and genuinely become a 'force for good' in our troubled world. Even so, we still have a hard job conveying the urgency with which they now need to move forward.

Is anybody too surprised encountering this moment of truth? Almost by definition, 'corporate sustainability' (or ESG, in its even less challenging mode) is a creature of capitalism as we know it today. A creature of Variant 1. It would never have been 'invited in' if that wasn't the case.

This conundrum has been laid bare in a new article from author and economist Duncan Austin (2021):

> "ESG aims to be a <u>solution</u> to our environmental and social challenges but is really a <u>symptom</u> of deeper cultural trends. As a market-based movement, it has had to uphold a market-friendly narrative, evident in some of its key refrains: 'win-win', 'doing well by doing good', and more. But the narrative that protecting the global environment must be profitable, and consistent with 'economic growth', seems increasingly implausible. ESG does not constitute 'ecological thinking', but rather the appropriation of some ecological concerns into a framework that remains steadfastly economic."

Conclusion – What Really Needs to be Done?

So, the inquiry shifts from 'How do we get rid of capitalism?' to 'How do we evolve our way out of these two inherently destructive variants of capitalism?' With an interesting subsidiary question: what is the role of multinational corporations today as highly influential players in today's global economy (and of all those invested in those multinational companies), in supporting that evolution?

Limited, inevitably, is the short answer to that question. Even the best of them, which are seriously engaged not just in minimising negative externalities but in increasingly significant 'force for good' interventions, are still constrained by the basic rules of the game. Profit maximisation, shareholder first, fiduciary duties: though these once iron-clad imperatives have all been softened as neoliberal capitalism's grip is loosened, that old rule book has not yet been officially set aside.

And there is, as yet, no consensus-based agreement as to what the new, future-fit variant of capitalism will look like. We don't even have any kind of mature discussion about the degree to which any new variant of capitalism will allow us to move beyond our obsessive pursuit of conventionally-measured economic growth. We all love parroting Joseph Stiglitz's mantra ('If we measure the wrong thing, we will do the wrong thing'), but there's still little concerted political will to grasp this particular nettle.

Which makes Professor Tim Jackson's new book, *Post Growth, Life after Capitalism* (2021, extremely timely as well and insightful:

> "Our prevailing vision of social progress is fatally dependent on a false promise: that there will always be more and more for everyone. Forged in the crucible of capitalism, this foundational myth has come dangerously unravelled. The relentless pursuit of eternal growth has delivered ecological destruction, financial fragility and social instability. We are trapped in an iron cage of consumerism. But the cage is of our own making. We are locked in the myth of growth. But the key was forged in our own minds. There are physical, material limits to our existence. But there is creativity in our souls that can free us to live meaningfully and thrive together."

That's the deeper work that has to start now if the basic precepts of a Green Economy are to be evolved into a rule book for tomorrow's capitalism.

About the Author

Jonathon Porritt, Founder Director of Forum for the Future, is an eminent writer, broadcaster and campaigner on sustainable development. He is Chancellor of Keele University and is involved in the work of many NGOs and charities as Patron, Chair or Advisor. He was Director of Friends of the Earth in the 1980s and chaired the UK Sustainable Development Commission 2000-2009. He received a CBE in January 2000 for services to environmental protection. His latest book, *Hope In Hell, A decade to confront the climate emergency*, was published by Simon and Schuster in 2020.

References

Austin, D. (2021), 'Can Economics Grasp What Ecology Says?', *Responsible Investor*, February 2021, **https://www.responsible-investor.com/reports/duncan-austin-or-can-economics-grasp-what-ecology-says**, accessed 30th March

Fancy, T. (2021), *Financial world greenwashing the public with deadly distraction in sustainable investing practices*, USA Today, 16th March **https://eu.usatoday.com/story/opinion/2021/03/16/wall-street-esg-sustainable-investing-greenwashing-column/6948923002/**, accessed 1st April

Gates, B. (2021), *How to Avoid a Climate Disaster: The Solutions We Have and the Breakthroughs We Need*, Allen Lane, London

Jackson, T. (2021), *Post Growth: Life after Capitalism*, Polity Press, Cambridge

Porritt, J. (2007), *Capitalism as If the World Matters*, Earthscan, Abingdon

Chapter Six

An Exploration Of Green Entrepreneurship, With Note To The Emerging UV-C Sterilisation Market

Tom Field, Chief Executive Officer, UVTech-Hygienics

Overview

This chapter explores the notions of being a 'green' business and discusses the differences this can have to green entrepreneurship. By deciphering between the two, this leads towards categorisation of businesses at different stages of adopting a green strategy and how this can be further harvested. Green entrepreneurship is then inspected in relation to the UV-C sterilisation industry and its positive environmental outcomes.

Introduction

As we understand more about the impact on the planet of our consumption decisions, the value of what's known as the 'green economy' increases. According to Sir David Attenborough "We have a responsibility to leave for future generations a planet that is healthy and habitable by all species" (BBC, 2002). This growing sense of collective responsibility will have a disproportionately negative impact on future generations. Fortunately, recognition of the impact of climate change on this planet is fuelling an increase in green entrepreneurship.

Green beans and Green machines

Within reason, every business has the opportunity to be 'greener' in their operations. This varies to different degrees depending on a host of factors. One of which is the variation between new and existing ventures. For the purpose of this analysis, this can be categorised into *green beans* and *green machines*. The first, green beans, is a business conception based around a greener and better solution for the environment (green entrepreneurship). The second, green machines, is a focus on resource and strategy around being a greener company, though may face limitations based on existing assets and output.

As a business, how you operate can be remodelled to have increased consideration for the environment and sustainable development. Concepts such as recycling protocols, digitising work streams, carbon footprint tracking, cycle to work schemes and contributing to re-planting programmes are just a few ways any business can become green machines. All these activities positively change the existing cultures and policies within an organisation for the better. However, existing businesses have the difficulty of not being easily able to change the essence of "what we do". In attaining strategic objectives, businesses are set up to achieve particular, commercially orientated, outcomes. Thinking about green objectives will not have been considered at the outset as part of strategy.

Because of the increase in green consciousness, there are companies whose green economic value has been re-evaluated. Such as a company who produces plastic bags for instance. Their operations might be green, but the limitation of their product prevents a totally green outcome. Through transitions in economic focus and awareness, traditional plastic bags are now considered to be an environmental hazard. Green entrepreneurship benefits from the fact a business at the development stage can explicitly address greener consciousness.

This is where green entrepreneurship becomes relevant. Green beans have the opportunity to consciously bring innovative and advanced ideas to market that are green from conception. An existing business may rethink their whole processes and operations to be greener. However, ultimately, if their output lacks opportunity for sustainable development, they are limited by output objectives not having been developed on a green model.

Exploring green entrepreneurship

Through my own experience and observations, green entrepreneurship is the practice of contributing towards the positive impact and engagement of sustainable living. Either through active thought leadership which guides the paths of other budding entrepreneurs, and, or delivering products and services that positively impact the environment at some point along the value chain. Or at the very least, reducing the negative impact that some parts of a business might have on the environment.

The weight to which an entrepreneur could then be classified as a green entrepreneur then ultimately depends on how central the focus of achieving green objectives is, as part of their everyday and long-term operations. The examination of green beans and green machines highlights the variations in green entrepreneurship at different stages of a business's development, and in addition these similar variations could also hold true when looking at green entrepreneurship exclusively. There is still a strong likelihood that even though a new entity could be considered a green bean, that actually having a "green" outcome is only a small part of the overall vision and objectives of the company.

For example, a new clothing company might look to have no packaging, reduce their waste and have a more positive impact on the environment. Compare this to that of a business who seeks to re-invent garments by using purely recyclable materials, offering a new sustainable type of clothing. Both ultimately have green intentions, but the latter example has adopted a wider green agenda which has more extrinsic implications. The difference being that the first example looks to bring intrinsic green value to the company by increasing their personal environmental impact, whereas the latter example offers a new consumer choice, changing the way we live to offer a more sustainable solution.

It's these extrinsically benefiting businesses which take a greater lead in the metamorphosis of our economy in becoming greener. Nevertheless it is important to note that all forms of green entrepreneurship carry value and should be celebrated, as it's that celebration which acts as the incentive for other businesses to adopt a green agenda. In simple economic terms though, the greener the agenda, the greater value this has to the green economy.

For green entrepreneurship to be harvested, there needs to be continued research and development into opportunities to innovate and change the way we use our resources. This comes from a multitude of sources including education, training, innovation centres and key policy which promotes, incentivises and advocates the development of green entrepreneurs. The 'arbitrator of success' is, as always, the marketplace. Indications are that customers respond positively to companies making a greener offer.

Green consumerism, based on increased ethical consumer spending, is increasing steadily and, in the last 20 years, as Smithers reports in The Guardian (2020), "Ethical consumer spending" on food, drinks, clothing, energy and eco-travel is now in excess of £41billion. Equally, there's been notable advances in sustainable based investment with around £2 trillion currently being invested into UK sustainable markets (Shehabi *et al*, 2019).

In addition, when looking at green machines, intrapreneurship within organisations should be fostered and celebrated to capitalise on the opportunities of existing businesses to reconsider their approaches to become greener. Through witnessing the rise of sub-groups in organisations such as employee councils and green committees, there is vastly increased scope for actionable change to be achieved.

It's through this celebration of green entrepreneurship and intrapreneurship on a macro and micro level which will ultimately act as the path towards an evolving economy. Economies don't change overnight and it takes wide adoption, reinforcement and incentive of ideas for that to happen. Any economic evolution is self-perpetuating, relying on the response of the marketplace which is clearly demonstrated above in that of the green economy. If the rate of consumer and investment interest continues on this trajectory, then this is arguably the greatest tool in successfully utilising green entrepreneurship as the lever in transitioning to a 'new' economy.

Setting up a green venture - UVTech-Hygienics

UVTech-Hygienics has benefited from introspection into a marketplace. Seeing the sterilisation market dominated with chemical-based solutions, we set up the company with the primary purpose of being a sustainable alternative to that of other resource intensive, environmentally challenging forms of sterilising. Our vision is that UV-C light can change the way we live and the way we protect ourselves from the transmission of bacteria and viruses.

Founded in July 2020, the company was born out of the challenges being faced due to the Covid-19 pandemic. Due to the pandemic, every business has been disrupted and in one way or another, had to adapt to the new world we live in. Offices have been closed for months on end, the increase in high street stores now offering click and collect, with businesses often having to follow their own industries infection control rules and regulations. In this time, the pandemic has highlighted the over-reliance we place on relatively unsustainable sterilisation methods. The likes of wipes, hand gels, disinfection sprays are resource intensive, throw-away, chemically based and even though effective in their role, arguably ineffective in their application due to being highly unsustainable.

UV-C light products offer a reusable resource with a lifespan of typically over 10,000 hours which aims to eradicate germs in a more natural manner. Not only is it a sustainable option in terms of net benefits to the environment, but also brings cost savings over time as it is a time-effective sterilisation method with some products being able to kill 99.9% of pathogens in a targeted area in seconds. Crucially, UV-C is able to operate through the achievement of sustainable outcomes.

UV-C light as the sustainable option

UV-C Light is a re-usable, long-lasting, green technology. It has been recognised as a sterilisation process technology since world war two in hospitals to sterilise medical equipment (Reed, 2010). It forms part of the ultraviolet spectrum and at certain wavelengths, optimally around 254nm, has the ability to agitate DNA and RNA creating crosslinks in the genetic structure of the pathogen and as a result, renders the bacteria or virus dead or inactive (Kowalski, 2010). This allows for a dry based sterilisation method which can kill 99.9% of viruses and bacteria, and one of the most effective methods in preventing the spread of infectious diseases (Reed, 2010).

As such, UV-C Light is nature's way to purify as there are no toxic by-products, bleaches or chemicals normally used when sterilising water either. This means that UV-C Light reduces the impact on the environment. The need to use significantly less bleaching agents may be achieved by ensuring water pumped into ecosystems is cleaned (Laville and McIntyre, 2020).

Though the emergence of UV-C is very much in the embryonic phase, the coronavirus pandemic has been a catalyst to increased awareness and application. For instance, UV-C Robots have been deployed at Heathrow Airport to sterilise their Terminals (BBC News, 2020), UV-C has been successfully trialled on the London Underground to sterilise the escalator handrails (Stone, 2020). UV-C is increasingly being used in contexts as varied as car keys, shopping centres, opticians, hotels, sports clubs and school classrooms. Additionally, for instance, by treating bread with UV light (Campden BRI, 2020) in its production process, it is possible to extend its shelf life. This creates opportunities for reduced wastage which, of course, is vital to the environmental effort. Our ambition is to further commercialise and domesticate the use of UV-C light thus ensuring green and sustainable benefits are more widely available to society.

UV-C may be used to extensively sterilise everything we come into contact with, and our shared indoor spaces, on a daily basis. Opportunities for UV-C sterilisation applications are truly endless. Our awareness of the destructive health and economic impact of the pandemic has alerted us to the importance of adoption of a technology with vast potential. Though UV-C will initially be used more extensively in medical infection control, having appliances which allow the technology to be of benefit to the general public will likely see a rapid rise in demand.

Driving successful green entrepreneurship

It requires incentive for any movement to gather momentum, and it is no different in this case of reflecting upon the adoption of green entrepreneurship. By the very nature of the phrase the "green agenda" the most compelling incentive of green entrepreneurship should be the positive impact on the environment. However, it is fair to say that the interest in green entrepreneurship can be inspired from sources more commercially advantageous. As discussed, the demonstration of the growing level of investment and consumerism in this sector is the most natural signalling factor to any entrepreneur to enter a market place. Entrepreneurship is fueled by the prospect of rewards; whether individually recognising or ultimately financially fruitful, and it is evident to see that on this basis the green economy offers this to entrepreneurs.

However, like any marketplace seeking adoption, there is going to be a varying combination of factors which motivate different groups of individuals to "adopt". In the same way an entrepreneur's motivation is driven by a different composition of objectives, thus creating incentives of different relative weights. Therefore any additional incentives required to further advocate a green agenda across businesses need to be in the vernacular of the entrepreneur; the impetus behind the evolving green economy.

Through time, these driving factors will change. None more so than the ability to measure the impact of sustainability which will naturally accumulate, developing further compelling evidence that supports the green agenda. For now, one of the best ways to signal the importance of the green agenda is through the green entrepreneurs of today sharing their visions through thought leadership. This activity is conducive to fostering green entrepreneurial communities that gradually leads towards "green clusters" of innovation hubs. Arguably, the biggest catalyst behind entrepreneurship is this collective entrepreneurial culture. Being able to be surrounded by a group of entrepreneurial thinkers, acts as great encouragement and reassurance to others to also foster similarly inspired business ventures. Any incentives which can allow budding entrepreneurs to unlock access to these types of surroundings would most definitely fuel greater appreciation of the green agenda.

The green entrepreneurs of today also arguably have more responsibility than your typical entrepreneur due to the underlying obligation to spread greater awareness and adoption. As a result, in these embryonic stages, a successful green entrepreneur is not necessarily one who just develops a sustainable venture. Success should arguably be judged with a wider lens, taking into consideration how actively one communicates the positive environmental impacts of their business, whilst also stimulating others to examine the sectors of industry they have interest in and offer them ways to recognise environmental deficiencies within those marketplaces.

As the proverb goes "necessity is the mother of invention" with the need in this instance, more than ever, being to protect the longevity of our planet. The roots of a new venture don't necessarily have to be green at heart; there will always be great merit in solving problems and improving the world we live in. But if those solutions can be grounded with sustainable concepts, then it will lead to some of the most productive forms of entrepreneurship.

Summary

The value of being green is growing steadily. Ultimately a 'green' business can come in many forms, shapes and sizes, to varying degrees. As explained, new businesses may form with the view of being green (green bean). Alternatively, existing business may become a green machine by embracing sustainable thought leadership and green intrapreneurship. Green entrepreneurs have the fortune of being able to conceive their business based on total green foundations from the outset. This goes all the way from conception to execution and the identity of the brand, in which customers respond to this signalling factor.

To bring both worlds together by a business becoming a 'green bean machine', an entity which is green from conception and operates sustainably, is arguably the best combination going forwards. In addition, UV-C Light offers a window into a market segment which is showing increased emergence due to its sustainable nature and relative benefits compared to alternatives. Wide-spread adoption of UV-C technology is set up to create positive environmental change as a result and should become a key part of infection control policy in the very near future.

About the Author

Tom Field runs operations for UV-C technology firm, UVTech-Hygienics which is based in the Birmingham area. UVTech-Hygienics provides UV-C light sanitisation solutions to disinfect air, water and surfaces. Customers have purchased products from an extensive range which includes large UV lamps to disinfect rooms, offices, warehouses and factories, to portable smaller boxes to insert phones, keys and even baby products. The comprehensive range caters to all types of settings and ensures a safe environment for individuals, employees and customers. Tom previously is a graduate of the University of Bath where he achieved a 1st class Honours degree in Business Administration.

References

BBC (2002), *BBC FOUR season marks Earth Summit*, BBC, 20th February, http://www.bbc.co.uk/pressoffice/pressreleases/stories/2002/08_august/20/bbcfour_earthsummit.shtml, accessed 26th March

BBC News (2020) 'Robots help fight coronavirus at Heathrow Airport', BBC Website https://www.bbc.com/news/av/technology-53525018, accessed 24th March

Campden BRI, (2021), 'UV Light tunnel', Campden BRI, https://www.campdenbri.co.uk/videos/uv-light-tunnel-system.php, accessed 26th March

Kowalski, W., (2010), Ultraviolet Germicidal Irradiation Handbook: UVGI for Air and Surface Disinfection, Springer Heidelberg Dordrecht, London

Laville, S. and McIntyre, N., (2020), 'Exclusive: water firms discharged raw sewage into England's rivers 200,000 times in 2019', Guardian, 1st July, https://www.theguardian.com/environment/2020/jul/01/water-firms-raw-sewage-england-rivers, accessed 30th March

Reed, N. G. (2010) 'The History of Ultraviolet Germicidal Irradiation for Air Disinfection', Public Health Reports, 125(1), pp. 15–27

Shehabi, S., Meade, R., Seath, M. and Lipkin, J., (2019). INVESTMENT MANAGEMENT IN THE UK 2018-2019. [ebook] London: The Investment Association (IA). Available at: <https://www.theia.org/sites/default/files/2019-09/IMS%20full%20report%202019.pdf> [Accessed 26 March 2021].

Smithers, R. (2020), 'UK ethical consumer spending hits record high, report shows', Guardian, 30th December, https://www.theguardian.com/environment/2019/dec/30/uk-ethical-consumer-spending-hits-record-high-report-shows, accessed 26th March

Stone, T., (2020), 'Covid-19: London Underground installs disinfecting UV lights on escalators', traffictechnologytoday.com, https://www.traffictechnologytoday.com/news/covid-19-news/covid-19-london-underground-installs-disinfecting-uv-lights-on-escalators.html, accessed 26th March

Chapter Seven

Making a Just and Fair Transition Work for All

Lisa Trickett and Bryan Nott, Co-Founders, Places in Common

Introduction

Whilst the pursuit of a green industrial revolution is politically seductive, and the efficacy of greening the economy is technically unchallengeable, the practicalities of delivering such an objective are not simple. The key policy imperative, acting now on climate change to avert crisis, does not attract universal support[1]. There is broad scientific agreement on climate change as a phenomenon (Cook, *et al*, 2016), but there is less scientific agreement about how to address it (Fawzy et al, 2020). Most people accept the existence of climate change, but there still remains dispute by those associated with so-called 'post truth' politics which impedes consent for the type of urgent and significant action that needs to be taken (Grafton and Kompas, 2020).

The existence of climate change and the challenge of securing public consent to act are products of the way in which society has been organised and governed to date. The green economy will not be delivered by maintaining thinking and approaches which have created the compelling need for new approaches. It may, we'd argue, be delivered by creativity, true collaboration, and by delivering a transition that is both just and fair to everyone.

The Competing Challenges of Climate Change

Addressing climate change is a complex issue but can be simplified to balancing three competing and interrelated factors. These are, the speed with which we need to transition to net zero carbon emissions, the level of impact on the economy and the level of impact on society. The close coupling and interrelationships mean that selecting one

---

[1] In a survey for Hope not Hate at the height of public action on climate change in September 2019, 74% of respondents strongly or partially agreed that the world was facing a climate emergency; see Hope Not Hate, (2019)

factor to be prioritised will directly impact the other two. Each factor has objective measures, a scientific assessment, which say, for climate is a 'tipping point'. Subjective measures, how we each feel about, for instance, the importance of a 'growing' economy, are influential. However, arguably, to date, avoiding an adverse impact on the economy and society has been the reason there's been insufficient urgency around securing a change to the current approach which has proven so destructive to the environment.

In debate concerning a green transition, there has been a tendency to focus on the economy in conjunction with varying timescales to achieve 'net zero'. This has been evident in the response of government but also in a wide range of actors from the trade union movement to the finance sector. Green jobs are vitally important, will benefit many, and very likely may form part of a route to net zero. They will not address inequalities across society more broadly. Indeed, there is a danger they will be part of a transition increasing inequality.

It is perhaps easier to decide the extent to which there is scope to safely act on the issues of the economy and the timing of action to address climate change. There are multiple ways in which the health and performance of the economy is measured, growth of GDP (gross domestic product) typically being paramount (Office for National Statistics, 2021). Equally a view can be taken about the consequences of achieving net zero by a given date (see Climate Change Committee, 2021). The social consequences and impact of action taken to avert climate change is harder to gauge and may be a reason why issues of social equity do not feature as prominently in the debate.

In terms of inequality, it's certainly the case that over a decade of austerity, coupled with a longer-term trend of technological and organisational changes in the economy, have left large parts of society far more vulnerable to adverse economic impacts than previously. This has led to a deterioration in social cohesion. As Jaccard (2020) believes, though the starting point of social cohesion is not always seen as relevant to the issue of action on climate change, taking it into account, in our view, is critical to the success of any plan. The reality is that the least well off in society, compared to those better able to absorb the consequences of investment in a green economy, face a triple injustice. Despite not being primarily responsible for climate change, this part of society may be required to bear a substantial proportion of the cost of addressing it. They are also likely to experience a significant increase in levels of inequality following any transition to net zero (Cook, et al, 2012).

Climate Change and Culture Wars

We have already seen action on climate change feature heavily as an issue leveraged by populist political actors (Lockwood, 2019; Gardiner, 2019). Populism does not simply target poorer communities, but seeks to capture a feeling amongst many that, for too long, successive governments have imposed solutions on behalf of a so-called 'liberal elite'. People from a wide cross section of economic statuses have embraced such a narrative although a central theme of populism, which can be summarised as "we're not going to take it any longer", readily appeals to those who've experienced deterioration in personal circumstances. That action on climate change is being brought with a catalogue of injustices used by the 'populist right' threatens to undermine any debate on what needs to be done.

Injustice and inequality are seen most clearly in the long-term freeze, effectively, because of inflation, a cut, in fuel duty. The actions of the French *gilets jaunes* damaged the prospects of a return to a gradual incremental increase in fuel duty there. At the same time, those who cannot afford a car have seen costs of public transport far outstripping the cost of car travel (Burke, 2019). This makes this form of mobility feel out of reach further cementing endemic disparity. If it is not possible to remove the sense of injustice and inequality possessed by many before addressing climate change, a compelling case should be made that such blights will be explicitly included as part of addressing it.

Part of the problem in building a consensus on action needed to address climate change is the lack of knowledge and awareness by the public. Those seeking to communicate a clear and urgent message have to compete with opposing voices such as the populist right who may not seek to win arguments, but merely to 'muddy waters' in any debate (Proctor and Schiebinger, 2008). Despite this, longstanding poll tracking reflects a shift in the perceived importance of the environment as an issue in recent years. As recently as June 2017, only 7% of respondents informed YouGov that the environment was one of the top three issues facing the country (YouGov, 2021a). The current equivalent figure is 29% (YouGov PLC, 2021b).

Whilst the perceived importance of the environment has improved, there is much less consensus about steps needed to be taken. Public support for particular measures remains uncertain. Last year the Climate Assembly UK published a range of measures required to ensure a net zero position (2020). It's notable the proposals were produced after intensive work over a series of six weekends, a level of engagement which would be difficult if not impossible to reproduce with the wider public though, for example, what's known as Citizens' Juries which has been used extensively in other European Countries. Whilst the Climate Assembly UK made some compelling recommendations, only one-third of the participants believed "urgency" in response to climate change should be a priority. The group also voted in favour of maintaining the Government's 2050 target for net zero. This tells us that if members of the public with a decent level of information and with support for action indicate hesitancy in acting with greater urgency, the prospect of building consent amongst the wider population remains a significant challenge.

Logically, it should be easier to garner consent for a just transition than for one that's lacks any commitment to greater justice and equality. Nonetheless, the components of such a transition remain unclear. This may be a reason why certainty of public support for climate change remains less than ideal. Building clearer consent for a just transition will entail policies intended to overcome the emotional responses of the public and does not ask them to place what are perceived to be long-term priorities over short-term day to day concerns. Unfortunately, public education in isolation will not achieve a sufficient shift in attitude.

There will always be some adhering to populist or anti-establishment narratives. However, those for whom the need to address climate change is a matter of balancing immediate challenges with longer-term issues, including fairness and redistribution, are crucial to success. Poorer communities are no less concerned about the environment than the better off and, historically, have frequently been at the forefront of action to deal with pollution, health and open spaces (Bell, 2020). The interests of such communities tending to focus on local or personal issues. This reflects, it may be speculated, their view of what comprises their 'sphere of influence' and the extent of their choice and control. A strategy to address climate change, to gain acceptance amongst those who perceive themselves to be disadvantaged and suffering inequality, needs to address more immediate concerns.

Finding a Sustainable Way Forwards

Simply compensating the less well off in relation to the impact of carbon-related regulation or pricing does not address issues of mistrust with a potential concern being that such compensation may be subject to political whim in the future and be rescinded (Carattini et al, 2018). Retraining and reskilling, which feature heavily in debate concerned with the green economy, has an important role to play. However, initiatives may fail to reach those not currently employed and may also be hampered if, ultimately, there's a net loss of jobs resulting from technological advances of a transition to a greener economy (Räthzel and Uzzell, 2011).

Dealing with structural inequality and increasing financial pressures experienced by people, particularly those with limited resources, to take on care for the young, the sick and the old, would go some way to dealing with the consequences from only focussing on compensatory measures and retraining (Cook, *et al, ibid*). Some of that may entail a debate about the nature of work and consumption. It was once the case that society was promised that the advance of technology would give rise to much greater leisure time. The reality, sadly, is that people are now working harder and longer with significantly reduced job security. A just transition needs to entail not just a redistribution of wealth within society, but the choice and control that wealth usually affords.

It is not just within communities that the impact of a period of austerity has been felt. Public authorities are much less well equipped in terms of resources and finance than they've been for generations. Consequently, their ability to respond to any major shifts in priorities is undermined. COVID and the pandemic has exposed the seriously weakened state of local government with the National Audit Office in 2021 noting the impact of a lack of long-term financial planning, the retrenchment to provision of core (typically care and safeguarding services), and the underlying vulnerability of authorities' finances (National Audit Office, 2021).

Achieving net zero will involve significant planning and action at a local, as well as national, level. This requires a strategic capacity that's largely been stripped out of local government. Even were such capacity an optimal level, there is a need for a shift in mindset in terms of policy assumptions and approaches. Understanding the legacy challenges of past transitions, the assets and resources that are available for harnessing, the competing priorities, relationships, drivers and interdependencies of different places and communities, will need to be part of an effective and just transition. The primary role of government has had too much focus on de-risking the scope for private investment and needs to recapture spirit of municipal activism of the 19th century (Shea Baird *et al*, 2019). Procurement processes are beset with limitations justified on the basis of 'what the market will bear' without a counterbalancing with what communities will bear or what's in their interest[1].

Conclusion

Building a transition that will be just and fair is going to need a pooling of knowledge, capacity and resources that has been evident in some of the response to the COVID pandemic. That the potential to do so exists should be used as a catalyst for any change in approach. Government at all levels needs to be creative and part of that creativity should be to address the imbalance between communities that has become embedded through past transitions (Mazzucato, 2021).

If a shared mission to act on the risk of climate change is to be fostered, it needs to achieve a wide and deep acceptance across communities, whether robust or weakened. It also needs to operate across spatial scales and sectors and spheres of government in a way that fosters a collaborative approach. Critical to success will be recognition of the huge variation in different communities' ability to absorb the impact of a zero-carbon transition. Therefore, it's essential to build into such a transition the structural changes addressing such inequalities as a central part of the overall mission.

About the authors

Lisa Trickett has held leadership positions in the sphere of public policy in both a political and professional context for over two decades. Lisa has worked within the public, private and higher educational sectors. She developed the Leadership of Place programme, whilst working with the University of Birmingham, which sought to create long term sustainable and inclusive communities through organisations of every kind working together. Lisa is currently a

---

[1] Permitted development rights and exemption from affordable housing are a key example, see, for example, Sagoe (2019)

Member of Birmingham City Council and served four years as the Cabinet Member for environmental and sustainability policy.

Bryan Nott spent over 25 years practising as a solicitor in the field of Public Law, Legal Aid and Trade Unions and headed a division of a national law firm. He co-founded Places in Common, a co-operative working in the field of climate change and securing a just transition. He has an MA from Ruskin College in International Labour and Trade Union Studies. He is a trustee of the Public Law Project, a national charity and has worked extensively with community groups in the field of social justice.

References

Bell, K., (2020), *Working-Class Environmentalism*, Springer International Publishing, Bristol

Burke, J., (2019), 'Neglect of duty: Why cutting fuel duty is incompatible with a net-zero UK'. (Blog), *Grantham Research Institute on Climate Change and the Environment*, 3rd September, https://www.lse.ac.uk/granthaminstitute/news/neglect-of-duty-why-cutting-fuel-duty-is-incompatible-with-a-net-zero-uk/, accessed 6 April 2021

Carattini, S., Carvalho, M. and Fankhauser, S., (2018), 'Overcoming public resistance to carbon taxes', *Wiley Interdisciplinary Reviews: Climate Change*, vol. 9(5), pp 531-556

Climate Assembly UK, (2020), *The Path to Net Zero Climate Assembly UK Full Report*, House of Commons, London

Climate Change Committee, (2021), *Reaching Net Zero in the UK*, Climate Change Committee, **https://www.theccc.org.uk/uk-action-on-climate-change/reaching-net-zero-in-the-uk/** accessed 6th April 2021

Cook, J., Oreskes, N., Doran, P., Anderegg, W., Verheggen, B., Maibach, E., Carlton, J., Lewandowsky, S., Skuce, A., Green, S., Nuccitelli, D., Jacobs, P., Richardson, M., Winkler, B., Painting, R. and Rice, K., (2016), *Consensus on consensus: a synthesis of consensus estimates on human-caused global warming, Environmental Research Letters*, 11(4), p.048002.

Cooke, B. and Kothari, U., (2002), *Participation, the new tyranny?*, Zed, London

Cook, S., Smith, K. and Utting, P., (2012), *Green economy or green society?*, UNRISD, Geneva

Fawzy, S., Osman, A., Doran, J. and Rooney, D., (2020), 'Strategies for mitigation of climate change: a review', *Environmental Chemistry Letters*, vol 18(6), pp.2069-2094.

Gardiner, B. (2019), *For Europe's Far-Right Parties, Climate Is a New Battleground*, Yale Environment 360, 29th October, **https://e360.yale.edu/features/for-europes-far-right-parties-climate-is-a-new-battleground?utm_campaign=Carbon%20Brief%20Daily%20Briefing&utm_medium=email&utm_source=Revue%20newsletter**, accessed 6th April 2021

Grafton. Q. and Kompas, T. (2020), *Tackling climate change in a 'post-truth' world - Policy Forum*, Policy Forum, https://www.policyforum.net/tackling-climate-change-in-a-post-truth-world/, accessed 6th April 2021

Hope Not Hate (2019), *Hopenothate.org.uk*, available at https://www.hopenothate.org.uk/wp-content/uploads/2019/09/HNH-International-Climate-Poll_Data-Tables-190919.zip, accessed 6th April 2021

Jaccard, M. (2020), *The Citizen's guide to climate success*, Cambridge University Press, Cambridge

Lockwood, M. (2019), 'Right-Wing Populism and Climate Change Policy', *Oxford Research Group*, https://www.oxfordresearchgroup.org.uk/blog/right-wing-populism-and-climate-change-policy, accessed 31st March 2021

Mazzucato, M., (2021), *Mission economy*, Allen Lane, London

National Audit Office, (2021), Local Government Finance, National Audit Office, London

Office for National Statistics, (2021), *Understanding the UK economy – Office for National Statistics*, https://www.ons.gov.uk/economy/nationalaccounts/articles/dashboardunderstandingtheukeconomy/2017-02-22, accessed 6th April 2021

Proctor, R. and Schiebinger, L. (2008), *Agnotology*, Stanford University Press, Stanford, California

Räthzel, N. and Uzzell, D. (2011), 'Trade unions and climate change: The jobs versus environment dilemma', *Global Environmental Change*, vol 21(4), pp.1215-1223

Sagoe, C. (2019), *Permitted development scandal: homeless families put at risk*, Shelter, https://blog.shelter.org.uk/2019/04/permitted-development-scandal-homeless-families-put-at-risk/, accessed 6th 2021

Shea Baird, K., Junque, M., En Comu, B., Bookchin, D. and Colau, A. (2019), *Fearless Cities: A guide to the global municipalist movement*, New Internationalist Publications Ltd, Spain

YouGov, (2021a), 'The most important issues facing the country', *Yougov.co.uk*, https://yougov.co.uk/topics/politics/trackers/the-most-important-issues-facing-the-country, accessed 6th April 2021

YouGov, (2021b), 'Top Issues Tracker (GB)', *Yougov.co.uk*, https://d25d2506sfb94s.cloudfront.net/cumulus_uploads/document/s7d4bpxjcw/YG%20Trackers%20-%20Top%20Issues_W.pdf, accessed 6 April 2021

Part Two
Principles in Action

Chapter Eight

The implications of decarbonisation for regional identities: can the centre hold?

Mathew Rhodes, Chair of West Midlands Energy Capital

Overview

In an increasingly decarbonised world, distinctive regional advantages will matter more. The economic, social and political geography of the UK changed significantly as the agricultural economy gave way to the fossil-fuel-powered industrial economy of the eighteenth, nineteenth and twentieth centuries. In this chapter we explore the idea that the transition to a green economy will have an equally profound impact.

Established approaches to regional development won't work any more

In the carbon age, sub-national regions have become used to developing industrial and economic strategies in standard ways. In countries like the UK, which is a relatively small island with well-developed infrastructure, we assume goods and people can move across the globe effortlessly and at minimal cost; we assume energy is universally available and cheap; and we assume people can live and work anywhere. The collective impact of these assumptions is that distinctive regional identities and capabilities lose their relevance to industrial and economic policy, and are retained only insofar as individuals find them socially comforting or politically-convenient. Even these residual roles of physical regions can easily be challenged by competing social identities, often now provided virtually and independent of geography (Wood, Solomon and Solomon, 2009).

However, such assumptions disguise the fact that modern industrial societies were built without any account for the environmental costs of carbon emissions. If society starts to count the costs of the carbon emitted into the atmosphere, we may find some of these unspoken assumptions which shape our society challenged. This in turn could have some interesting implications for regional and national strategies and identities. This chapter makes some preliminary suggestions as to what these implications might be.

How a decarbonised economy will change the rules

A decarbonised economy, the desired outcome of policies which account accurately for the costs of carbon emissions, will change the assumptions underpinning industrial strategies and national economic policy making in multiple ways.

Firstly, the energy that powers economies will start to come from new places. This will potentially have geopolitical implications as well as implications within national economies. For the UK, it means the value of local coal, oil and gas reserves and the technologies to exploit these will diminish unless the associated carbon emissions can be captured and reliably and economically stored. The value of renewable resources such as offshore wind will rise. Both carbon capture and storage and large-scale renewables (including nuclear power) only work economically in a limited number of places: geologically-stable undersea reservoirs are needed for carbon storage and coastal locations are required for large scale renewables and nuclear power.

Secondly, there will be more constraints on where energy can economically be used. In the twentieth century, we moved away from societies being tied to the locations where fuel was readily available because we developed a transport infrastructure, itself powered by fossil fuels, which could transport fuels to the locations where society and economies needed to transform them into useful power, including individual internal combustion engines and (in the UK) individual domestic heating systems. This meant, for example, that economies in the Middle East could be built on oil even though markets for these resources were elsewhere in the world. In a decarbonised economy, the primary power source (electricity) will largely be generated where the wind blows and the sun shines, and any remaining carbon-intense heat and power (for example required by high temperature industrial processes) will need to be generated where the carbon emissions can be captured and stored economically. This means a limited number of locations (adjacent to the North and Irish Seas in the UK).

Power transmission and distribution networks – electricity infrastructure in particular – will matter more, and transport infrastructure will matter less. The decision on whether to build a national hydrogen infrastructure to replace the gas network becomes a significant one: it's not clear that the national benefits exceed the costs because the alternatives (widely electrified heating and transport, and local district energy networks) often make better economic sense for most energy demands in cities and are widely deployed across the world.

Finally, the way the economy works will change. When the amount of carbon embodied in products (and services) is measured and valued, as the UK government is beginning to propose (BEIS, 2021) this incentivises more circular approaches. Demand-side policies such as carbon taxes and labelling of products with embodied carbon values will encourage companies to maximise use of locally-available resources. This will include making use of local waste streams, and also encouraging redesign of products and services for re-use, more sharing of infrastructure and minimisation of transport costs (Braungart and McDonough, 2002).

The combination of these factors has the potential to shift the balance of power within and between nations. We need to start thinking about national and regional economic and industrial strategies in new ways.

Emerging regional roles in a decarbonised world

There will be four kinds of region in a decarbonised world: firstly, regions with historic fossil fuel resources which also have lots of renewables (the north east of England and Scotland for example); secondly, regions with no historic energy resources, but which turn out to have relatively plentiful renewables (Cornwall's access to solar energy in the UK context is in this category); thirdly, regions which have neither fossil fuels nor renewables (for example, London and the South East); and fourthly, regions with a history of access to fossil fuels but with very limited renewable resources (the West Midlands). Each of these categories of region faces a different challenge in transitioning to a decarbonised economy.

Regions with access both to fossil fuel and renewables are likely to be the industrial hubs of the future, particularly if they are well-populated. Their populations mean they have significant local demand for products and services as well as energy. Old oilfields are also viable locations for carbon capture and storage, although this requires significant investment in pipelines and therefore is only economically-viable for energy generation nearby (Gonzales, Krupnik and Dunlap, 2020). In some ways, therefore, for regions like the north of England the transition to a decarbonised economy may represent potential for a rediscovery of a role and identity which they last experienced in the late nineteenth century, before globalisation destroyed their relative competitive advantages.

Regions with no historic energy resources but plentiful renewables, such as Cornwall, and also those built more recently on fossil fuels (Alaska, the Middle East, Scotland) are typically less well populated. They face similar opportunities in principle, but without the population to provide a captive local market they will either need investments in infrastructure to enable them to sell the clean power they can generate, or they will need to attract significant populations to use this clean power locally.

For regions with neither fossil nor renewable resources the challenges are more subtle, but significant. Where a regional economy has been built on trade and finance, like London, the challenge will be dealing with potential structural changes in global trade patterns as economies become more circular and localised (Dellink, 2020). There will be a heavy reliance on virtual technologies, and the need to secure access to clean electricity and heat will drive a need to collaborate with or to control neighbouring regions.

Potentially the most challenged regions, though, are those like the West Midlands with regional economies which have been shaped by fossil fuels but which have no substantive local renewable resource base. Without significant investment in infrastructure, in a decarbonised world a traditional industrial strategy makes much less economic sense. The population faces a difficult choice between relocating or reskilling. The kind of economy which supported this type of region through much of the twentieth century simply isn't viable in a decarbonised world - at least not without significant ongoing subsidy - so there is a need to find a new role and new strategic approach entirely. This is likely to be particularly challenging when the industrial economy has shaped the local culture and identity, as it clearly has in the West Midlands (Money, 1977).

Pursuing the West Midlands example further, the immediate choice seems to be between a stronger partnership with the South East or development of new industrial models focused on less energy-intense manufacturing. For example, this might mean adopting circular economy principles or emphasising knowledge-based sectors such as data, communications, entertainment, healthcare or life sciences.

A strategy of stronger partnership with the South East is supported by new transport and communications infrastructure investments already underway, such as HS2 and 5G, but this approach may face cultural and practical challenges and potential social upheaval because it implies a loss of what remains of the region's identity and culture. In contrast, transitioning the West Midlands' industrial economy into new sectors and adopting circular economy principles fits much better with the existing regional culture and sense of identity. However, it will require a recognition from existing institutions and anchor employers that defending a traditional industrial status quo is no longer viable and that significant industrial and supply chain reconfiguration will be necessary.

Can the centre hold?

Erosion of distinctive regional identities has been characteristic of the past two centuries in the UK (Kenny, McLean and Paun, 2018). However, a decarbonised world is fundamentally more localised, so there is an opportunity for regional boundaries to gain definition and significance once more. Indeed, as we've outlined here, regional interests will potentially start to diverge depending on their geographical assets and historical strengths. This tendency can be offset to a degree by investment in shared energy, transport and communications infrastructure, but this infrastructure will be expensive. The way costs are distributed may well be contested and a source of ongoing tension: why should industry in one region be handicapped in competing globally because it is paying for infrastructure to keep a population in another region which might be more productively employed if it migrated north (for example)?

Ultimately, it may be wiser, as well as cheaper, to welcome the strengthening and divergence of regional identities and industrial interests that decarbonisation implies. The clear implication of this argument, however, is that in a decarbonised world the centre – national government in particular – is going to have to learn how to think and work differently. Ignoring regional identities and distinct interests has been possible in our fossil-fuelled economy, but this will be much less viable in future. Perhaps a more federal and partnership-based approach might work better, where each region recognises the relative strengths and distinctive advantages of the others and the centre holds the ring in everyone's interests. Will this work in UK political culture? Given the UK's history of heavily centralised government, which stretches back well into medieval times, this seems a little unlikely, but then we do live in strange times.

About the author

Matthew Rhodes is Chair of West Midlands Energy Capital, the regional energy infrastructure partnership accountable to the Mayor and supported by the regional electricity and gas distribution networks. He's worked at the interface of academic research and commercial deployment in the low carbon sector for over 25 years and was until recently a Board member of the Greater Birmingham and Solihull Local Enterprise Partnership.

References

BEIS (2021). UK Industrial Decarbonisation Strategy

Dellink, R. (2020), "*The consequences of a more resource efficient and circular economy for international trade patterns: A modelling assessment*", OECD Environment Working Papers, No. 165, OECD Publishing, Paris

Braungart, M., and McDonough, W., (2002) Cradle to Cradle: Remaking the Way we Make Things. London: Vintage.

Gonzales, V., Krupnik, A., Dunlap, L., (2020) Carbon Capture and Storage 101, Resources for the Future, https://www.rff.org/publications/explainers/carbon-capture-and-storage-101/ [accessed May 27 2021].

Kenny, M., McLean, I., Paun, A., (2018) Governing England: English Identity and Institutions in a Changing United Kingdom. Oxford: Oxford University Press.

Money, J (1977) Experience and Identity: Birmingham and the West Midlands, 1760-1800. Manchester: Manchester University Press.

Wood, N.T., and Solomon, M.R., (2009) Virtual Social Identity and Consumer Behaviour. London: Routledge.

Chapter Nine

Growing Digital Economy and Connectivity for a Net Zero Age

Margot James, Executive Chair, WMG
Hopi Sen, Research Fellow, WMG
Dr Vannessa Goodship Associate Professor, Materials and
Manufacturing Group, WMG, University of Warwick

Overview

The role of digitisation in achieving a carbon neutral economy is a complex interaction of political, societal, and economic transformation which crosses many traditional international and sector boundaries. To achieve our net zero goals, we need to deliver on the potential of digitisation to reduce carbon emissions by greening energy systems, reducing energy demand in industry, transport and home settings, while reducing the energy cost of data and ensuring a zero-waste approach to computing and digital technologies. All of this requires investment in the infrastructure and skills needed to ensure digitisation contributes effectively to carbon elimination across the economy.

Digital Replacement of Carbon Emissions

We have now reached a digital age where technology not only aids our daily living but can enhance our experience of everyday reality. At the individual level, the COVID pandemic has accelerated acceptance of this new digital experience, while permanently changing the way we approach work and play. Similarly, the crisis has provided an opportunity for enhancing and popularising many software platforms previously not used widely on the internet and showcased the power that can be harnessed by big data collection and augmented reality.

However, the consequence of digitisation has the potential to have far broader impact, supporting a digital transformation of both industry and society, which, if managed well, will help deliver the net zero carbon objectives set out in the Paris Climate Change accords. For example, the switch to remote working and digital networks can offer one solution to our growing (offline) energy consumption demands, as commuting by road, rail or air, and many social activities can be replaced by digital alternatives. This can reduce the need for energy consumption in households and industry, whether through the use of sensors to manage energy demand, reducing the energy usage of industrial operations, supporting the effective utilisation of renewable energy sources or the effective management of grids.

It has been estimated that digital technology already in application could reduce global carbon emissions by up to 15 per cent (Deloitte and TechUK, 2020). A document prepared by PwC for Microsoft states "[AI would] contribute up to USD 5.2 trillion to the global economy in 2030 and create 38.2 million net new jobs across the world" (PwC UK, 2019). However, it is clear there is still some way to go to meet these targets. To deliver on the potential for digitisation in greening our energy infrastructure or the ability of digital manufacturing to reduce carbon emissions in the production, use and re-use of products, there are two key issues which need to be addressed. The first is ensuring the sustainability of digitisation itself, whether the energy consumed by digital processes or in the production of digital goods. The second is the innovation, skills and data framework that will encourage households and businesses to make necessary changes to their existing habits in order to reduce energy demands.

Greening Energy systems and Industry through Digitisation

Energy System Digitisation

Today, the National Grid uses a range of digital technologies to forecast energy supply and demand. By modelling the availability of different energy sources, and forecasting supply and demand across the entire system, technologies such as AI and digital twinning can help integrate intermittent renewable energy sources such as wind, solar and nuclear energy into the grid [National Grid ESO, 2021] in line with consumer demand. We have already seen digital twins developed for wind farms, helping to optimise the design of wind turbines for specific sites. Once the turbines are operating, the digital twin then supports their operation and maintenance remotely, helping to improve efficiency, improving operations, and according to one recent study, the twin could increase the annual energy production of a wind farm by up to 20 per cent. (Royal Society, 2020).

In addition, the National Grid maintains large information data sets from around the UK, and data analytics can further aid the transformation to net zero, by supporting prompts to customers to make better decisions about their energy use. For example, Smart meters in households enable consumers to monitor and control their home energy demands and can be used to offer prompts to users whose consumption is higher than those in similar households or industries. Delivering digital improvements to smart metering, such as integration to household devices and phones and allowing intuitive remote control over systems will drive consumer demand for the technology. (Brightstar, 2021).

According to the International Energy Agency (IEA), implementing these kind of Smart demand responses alone would offer 185 GigaWatts of system flexibility globally, saving up to USD 270 billion in investment in new electricity infrastructure (International Energy Agency, 2017). At a system scale, open and transparent data on energy consumption will also permit more effective targeting of energy efficiency programmes, ensuring high energy consumption households are offered advice on insulation, boiler technology, heat pump and renewable energy installation in the home. (National Grid, 2021).

Industrial Digitisation

Current emissions from industry stem from initial material processes, such as the mining, refining, or synthesis of the required raw materials, such as steel and aluminium, and extend through entire associated supply chains involved in the manufacturing and subsequently sale of these items to the consumer. It is therefore not surprising that over 80 per cent of the carbon emissions associated with these devices come in the manufacturing stage, and that digitisation here can have significant impact on Carbon reduction. As the recent UK Government Industrial decarbonisation strategy says technologies such as 3D printing and digital twins can reduce product weights, extend life cycles and improve the cost-effectiveness, efficiency and flexibility of the production process. (Department for Business, Energy and Industrial Strategy, 2021).

For example, deploying Electro-Magnetic (EM) sensors in the production of steel can support less wasteful, higher throughput steel production, while Digital Twins, as in the energy sector, can reduce the energy demands of industry (Sustain, 2021) A national connected network of digital twins and greater data sharing is estimated to release an addition £7 Billion per year (Bolton et al, 2017).

Equally, the growth of the electric vehicle market highlights the need for effective recycling and reuse of Batteries and associated systems. A recent report by WMG (Sattar et al, 2020) modelled that by 2040, the UK will require 567,000 tonnes of cell production, requiring 131,000 tonnes of cathodic metals. Recycling can potentially supply 22 per cent of this demand (assuming a 60 per cent recycling rate and 40 per cent reuse or remanufacture). This could be supported by deploying sensors within battery cell which transmit information on battery status, both supporting a market for second-hand batteries by verifying the health of the battery and signposting potential for reuse, and by identifying the most appropriate recycling and re-use process. (European Commission, 2018).

Transport Systems

Digital technologies can also support the development of Net Zero mobility in other ways, both in optimising the use of existing physical infrastructure to reduce carbon demands and by reducing the carbon emissions of public and personal transport. Already, transport systems are being transformed as sensor technology enables smart motorways to control traffic flow and to map and control the location of individual vehicles. Changes in traffic laws, the expansion of 4G network coverage across all road networks, and a plan to enable safe deployment, are essential to the commercialisation of Autonomous vehicles (SMMT, 2019). Equally, by maintaining cloud-connected vehicles optimization of logistics, maintenance and manpower can be realized. Scania has 500,000 such cloud-connected vehicles on the road. (Björkdahl, 2020).

We are also seeing the emergence of 'mobility as a service' business models, which leverage digital technologies to increase the time in use of vehicles on the roads, reducing demand for personal vehicles and supporting models such as vehicle-sharing to limit road usage. Equally, in public transport, data-enabled transport services permit users to access, pay for, and get real-time information on public transport, supporting a modal shift to lower carbon modes of transport. (Government Office for Science, 2018).

As a recent report by the Connected Places Catapult has argued, there are clear carbon reductions to be achieved through the adoption of Connected and Autonomous vehicles (CAV), including using autonomy to support 'eco-driving techniques', shared occupancy, network efficiency and reduced powertrain size. However, without clarity in policy there are also potential risks for carbon increase, as the greater convenience and lower cost enabled by CAV could potentially increase the overall demand for mobility. (Kopelias et al, 2020). It is crucial, therefore, that policy and industry innovation is focussed on supporting the adoption of CAV in ways that support the objective of lower emissions, for example by supporting shared vehicle usage, mobility as a service and supporting the use of CAV in public transport and last mile freight deliveries. (Connected Places Catapult, 2020).

Reducing the Energy Demand of Digitisation and Data Storage

Advancing digitisation has meant an increasing number of digital devices. There are considerable carbon emissions associated with the hardware that supports digitalisation, the manufacture of electronic devices (mobile phones, computers, laptops, televisions, etc) as well as other manufactured items. Equally, at the end of life of electronic devices, there is considerable waste. In 2017, an average e-waste of 13.2kg/person was generated in the UK and the total amount of waste produced in the EU reached more than 9 million tons by 2020. (European Commission, 2020).

The required energy demand of all aspects of the manufacturing and end-of-life process can be reduced by advancing digitisation. The deployment of sensors in finished goods can enable tracking of the fate of all our electronic devices, supporting efforts to ensure recycling and reuse. One recent example of this is the use of robotics to support the disassembly of televisions, improving both the amount of material recovered and the economic value of the recovered materials. (Álvarez-de-los-Mozos et al, 2020).

Renewable Digitalisation

The storage and management of Data itself can also produce higher emissions. While the estimate in 2018 put data usage at 33 Zettabytes (ZB), the International Data Corporation forecasts the Global Datasphere to grow to 175 ZB by 2025 with potentially an associated increase in power consumption contributing to carbon emissions. (International Data Corporation, 2020). It is therefore imperative to also consider an associated reduction in energy demands that can be achieved by the results of advances in digital manufacturing and recycling in the physical world.

The demand for data centres has grown with internet usage and global IP traffic. Data levels have increased 10 times, since 2018, with storage capacity on global data centres following this increase by a further factor of 25. Maintaining all this data requires a considerable amount of cooling, and servers (and their cooling) require more energy consumption than the storage drives and network devices attached. As a guide, data centres used 1 per cent of the entire global electricity output in 2018, with 2 per cent of that based in the USA. (Masenet et al, 2020).

To ensure that digitisation itself is environmentally viable, there needs to be complete sustainability in all aspects of digitisation from networks, data storage, to software platforms. This includes both the energy consumption requirements of vast data storage and the development of more energy efficient data storage and processing technologies. A switch to entirely renewable energy sources is one solution, which has been rolled out amongst companies such as Google, Apple, and Facebook. A more creative solution is to consider how to use that generated heat, rather than simply just cool it. Capturing this wasted heat energy and using it to heat local homes for instance would reduce carbon emissions and total costs (Google, 2021).

Further reductions in emissions will come with innovations in computing devices and related technology. For example: between 2010-2018: there was a 6x increase in computing output, with a 6 per cent increase in power consumption. For Google, between 2015-2020, there was 7x increase computing power, with no change in power usage, this improvement is supported by new chip designs with 45 per cent greater efficiency than earlier designs.

Keys to deliverability

The potential of green digitalisation to reduce carbon emissions is significant. The Made Smarter Review found that the adoption of digitalisation technologies could reduce carbon dioxide emissions in manufacturing alone by 4.5 per cent without sacrificing economic growth in the sector. (Department for Business, Energy & Industrial Strategy ,2017) Based on the increasing capability of digital technologies, including AI, and increased accuracy of sensor systems, it is hoped that this will prove an underestimate.

To achieve this, the UK must first be equipped with a green and secure digital infrastructure that can underpin our zero-emission society. This will be achieved through digitisation that is fully embedded and able to enhance our power grid and supplied by a range of renewable sources, our autonomous green transport systems and our smart construction and housing.

Manufacturing industries must also embrace digitisation in advancing smart manufacturing. Whether in the development of smart industrial processes to reduce energy use or in the creation of low energy consuming and easily recycled digital products, policies must incentivise green digitisation.

To support this aim there is a need for a rapidly developing and flexible range of net zero skills that will be needed at all levels to train the next generation of data-driven digital innovators.

A national strategy for Net Zero digital must provide diversity and inclusiveness, access, and opportunities across socio-economic and demographic populations to digital skills and training with upskilling and reskilling available as part of that program. This requires monitoring and further action as needed. No one should be left behind.

How can we achieve this? As we have seen, there is a key role for innovation, industrial translation and skills development in supporting the broad adoption of green digitisation. Each of these steps requires a partnership between industry and research and skills providers, often at the firm level. There is therefore a need for a clear national strategy for deploying digital technology to support green industrialisation, and support for translational institutions to engage in digital knowledge and skills exchange to support the greening of our economy. For example, at WMG, we offer a Master's course in Sustainable Automotive Electrification, which contains modules on the modelling and simulation of systems and connected and autonomous vehicles.

As the sectors which can benefit from these technologies are as varied as energy infrastructure, materials, battery technology, circular economy and data centres, support for green digitisation needs to be embedded within existing industry partnerships, giving researchers, industry and educators the flexibility needed to address the specific challenges of their sector.

About the author

Margot James has had a wide-ranging career which has spanned parliament, government and entrepreneurship. Both in business and government Margot has championed the need to expand opportunities for diverse groups of young people. Margot served as Minister of State for the Department for Digital, Culture, Media and Sport, with responsibility for Digital, Telecoms and the Creative Industries, piloting the Data Protection Bill through Parliament, incorporating GDPR into UK law. Previously she served as Parliamentary Under-Secretary of State at the Department for Business, Energy and Industrial Strategy, with responsibility for small businesses, consumers and corporate governance, including labour markets. Margot co-founded Shire Health Group and led its growth to over 100 staff, having created a market for industry sponsored public health campaigns. She led the successful transitioning of Shire Health Group to the multinational WPP in 2000.

She served on the Europe, Middle East and Africa Board of Ogilvy Mather, leading European healthcare programmes.

References

Álvarez-de-los-Mozos, E,. Rentería-Bilbao, A. and Díaz-Martín, F. (2020) 'WEEE Recycling and Circular Economy Assisted by Collaborative Robots', *Applied Science*, vol. 10, 4800 pp 1-13 4800. Doi: 10.3390/app10144800

ARUP (2019) 'Digital twin, towards a meaningful framework', available from **https://www.arup.com/-/media/arup/files/publications/d/digital-twin-report.pdf,** accessed 8th May 2021

Björkdahl, J. (2020), 'Strategies for Digitalization in Manufacturing Firms', *California Management Review*, Vol. 62, Issue 4, pp 17-36, doi: 10.1177/0008125620920349

Bolton, A., Butler, L.., Dabson, I., Enzer, M., Evans, M., Fenemore, T., and Harradence, F. (2018) *Gemini Principles (CDBB_REP_006),* availlable online at https://doi.org/10.17863/CAM.3226 accessed 8th May 2021

Brighstar (2021), *Brighstar Insights,* available online at https://www.brightstar.com/insights/, accessed 17th May 2021

Connected Places Catapult (2020) *The CAV Decarbonisation Paradox,* Section 3.3-3.5, available from https://cp.catapult.org.uk/wp-content/uploads/2020/12/Connected-Places-Catapult-The-CAV-Decarbonisation-Paradox-report-November-2020-Copy.pdf, accessed 8th May 2021

Deloitte and TechUK (2020), *Making the UK a digital clean tech leader*, available online https://pixl8-cloud-techuk.s3.eu-west-2.amazonaws.com/prod/public/dc5d0fa9-7644-4178-a0e3bddc39d428f5/Making-the-UK-a-digital-clean-tech-leader-report.pdf, accessed 8th May 2021

Department for Business, Energy & Industrial Strategy (2017), *Made Smarter Review*, 30th October 2017, London

Department for Business, Energy and Industrial Strategy (2021), *Industrial Decarbonisation Strategy*, March 2021, CP399. HMSO, London

European Commission (2018), *Towards the battery of the future. Future Brief Issue 20*, available online at towards_the_battery_of_the_future_FB20_en.pdf (europa.eu), accessed 7th May 2021

European Commission (2020), *Eurostat Energy Transport and Environment Statistics , 2020 edition*, Luxembourg: Publications Office of the European Union, doi: 10.2785/522192

Google Data Centers (2021), *Renewable Energy*, available online at Renewable energy – Data Centers – Google, accessed 7th May 2021

Government Office for Science (2018) *Mobility as a Service (MaaS) in the UK: change and its implications*, available online at Mobility as a Service (MaaS) in the UK: change and its implications (publishing.service.gov.uk), accessed 8th May 2021

Kopelias, P., Demiridi, E., Vogiatzis, K., Skabardonis, A. and Zafiropoulou, V. (2020), *Connected & autonomous vehicles–Environmental impacts–A review, Science of the total environment*, 712, 135237, doi: 10.1016/j.scitotenv.2019.135237

International Data Corporation (2020, *Worldwide Global DataSphere Forecast, 2020–2024: The COVID-19 Data Bump and the Future of Data Growth* (Doc #US44797920), Summary available online at IDC's Global DataSphere Forecast Shows Continued Steady Growth in the Creation and Consumption of Data, accessed 8th May 2021

International Energy Agency (2017), *Digitalisation and Energy, IEA, Paris*, available online at **https://www.iea.org/reports/digitalisation-and-energy**, accessed 7th May 2021.

Masanet, E., Arman, S., Nuoa, L., Smith, S. and Koomey, J. (2020), *Recalibrating Global Data Center Energy Use Estimates, Science*, vol. 367, No. 6481 pp 984-986.

National Grid ESO (2021) *available online at Digitalising the grid: our ambition for harnessing data and technology*, National Grid ESO, accessed 7th May 2021

PwC UK (2019) *How AI can enable a sustainable future*, available online at **https://www.pwc.co.uk/services/sustainability-climate-change/insights/how-ai-future-can-enable-sustainable-future.html**, accessed 8th May 2021

Royal Society (2020), *Digital Technology and the Planet: Harnessing computing to achieve net zero*, ISBN: 978-1-78252-501-1, Issued: December 2020 DES7035, available online at Digital technology and the planet: harnessing computing to achieve net zero (royalsociety.org), accessed 8th May 2021

Sattar, A., Greenwood, D., Dowson, M. and Unadkat, P. (2020) *Automotive Lithium ion Battery Recycling in the UK*, WMG. Available online at **https://warwick.ac.uk/fac/sci/wmg/business/transportelec/22350m_wmg_battery_recycling_report_v7.pdf**, accessed 7th May 2021

SMMT (2019) Connected and Autonomous Vehicles, 2019 Report Available at https://www.smmt.co.uk/wp-content/uploads/sites/2/SMMT-CONNECTED-REPORT-2019.pdf, date accessed 7 May 2021

Sustain (2021) available at *SUSTAIN Steel - EPSRC Future Steel Manufacturing Research Hub*, accessed 7th May 2021

Bibliography

Chan, P. H., , Dhadyalla, G. and Donzella, V. (2020), 'A framework to analyze noise factors of automotive perception sensors', *IEEE Sensors Letters*, Vol. 4, No. 6 pp. 1-4. doi:10.1109/LSENS.2020.2996428

Espineira, J., Robinson, J., Groenewald, J., Chan, P.H. and Donzella, V. (2021), 'Realistic LiDAR with noise model for real-time testing of automated vehicles in a virtual environment final', *Sensors Journal*. pp. 1-8. doi:10.1109/JSEN.2021.3059310

Goodship, V., Stevels, A.B. and, Huisman, J. [eds] (2019), *Waste electrical and electronic equipment (WEEE) handbook, 2nd Edition*, Woodhead Publishing, Oxford, UK

Groenewald J., Grandjean, T., Marco, J., Widanage, D. (2017), 'Testing of Commercial Electric Vehicle Battery Modules for Circular Economy Applications', *SAE International Journal of Materials and Manufacturing*, vol. 10, No. 2 pp. 206-17.

SAE International (2021), *Standard J3016_202104, Taxonomy and Definitions for Terms Related to Driving Automation Systems for On-Road Motor Vehicles*, SAE International, Warrendale, PA, USA

Sommerville, R., Shaw-Stewart, J., Goodship, V., Rowson, N. and Kendrick, E. (2021), 'A review of physical processes used in the safe recycling of lithium ion batteries', *Sustainable Materials and Technologies*, e00197 2021

The 3xD Simulator for Intelligent Vehicles, available online at https://www.youtube.com/watch?v=dhUy-ikmM4s , date accessed 9 May 2021

WMG (2021), Available online at WMG - The University of Warwick, accessed 7th May 2021

See for details of teaching from our academies, apprenticeships through to postgraduate qualifications, for of our leading industry relevant research activities and how we work with business.

Chapter Ten

Building our Zero Carbon Economy on Green Foundations

Tor Farquhar, Ex-Executive Director of HR and IT, Tata Steel Europe

Overview

How developing a zero-carbon economy, built with 'green' steel, can ensure a renaissance for manufacturing in the UK. This will create lasting social impact from sustainable high-value jobs in areas where they are needed. This requires radical changes in all sectors. The challenge is to achieve greener manufacturing whilst maintaining and enhancing living standards.

Transition points in the UK economy

The key sectors in which change will be needed:

Energy including development through offshore wind, nuclear power and hydrogen to replace carbon-based fuel demand for heat, light and transportation. This requires 'lock-in' energy diversity to support the demand for electricity and carbon capture utilisation and storage.

Transportation in which utilisation of electric vehicles rapidly increases. There will be conversion of internal combustion engines for high torque applications, LGV, HGV and 'Yellow Goods' through biodiesel to hydrogen as technology and infrastructure develop. Integrated intelligent cities included far greater propensity to walk and cycle as well as combined with zero carbon rail, electric trains with battery capacity. More generally, 'jet zero' and green marine, provide significant challenges.

Construction will need zero emission housing as well as all buildings being inter-connected power stations, each applying an array of micro-generation technologies, coupled with a transformative retrofit of 23 million existing homes. This will need durable and recyclable materials such as steel and glass and far superior insulation reducing energy waste (and overall consumption) thereby making UK households safer, more comfortable, and providing cost saving.

Industry removal of carbon as a fuel source and the technologies to achieve this using renewable electricity and green hydrogen, is essential. Removal of carbon from chemical processes where it acts as a reductant, provides a more complex, yet manageable challenge. The introduction of carbon into molecular structures in a responsible manner poses a more significant technical challenge.

Nature and Agriculture the biodiversity crisis, loss of soil health, public health issues linked to obesity and deteriorating mental health, as well as the threat of water scarcity and flooding pose significant social and environmental challenges. These need carefully planned responses including tree planting, responsible forestry, rewilding and targeted de-intensification of unsustainable practices. Equally, expansion of digital and automation into arable farming will potentially transform efficiency, skills and resilience as well as reducing harmful emissions.

Services it's essential to capitalise on progress in delivering a balanced zero-carbon economy through the sales globally of consulting in areas such as connected spaces, workforce and societal mobility, intelligent cities and financial services.

The Current Economy – some insights from steel

Steel is an essential component for all manufacturers and construction developments being used in almost everything we can think of. In 2018, UK manufacturing output was £186 billion, 10% of total UK economic output. Developed economies are naturally steel intensive; every year the UK consumes 260kg of steel per person. In steel we already have the ideal material for delivering a lower-impact society. Steel can endlessly be recycled. Steel costs less than competitor materials and costs approximately 75% of aluminium and 18% of carbon fibre. Traditionally steel is manufactured in a way contributing to climate change through carbon emission, Consequently, radical change has been necessary for if to continue to play a role in the green economy. Notably, the IEA (International Energy Agency) predict global demand for steel by 2050 will exceed 2 billion tonnes. The UK government believe domestic demand will grow by 10% to 11 million tonnes by the end of the decade, driven specifically by the need for new 'low-carbon products.

Such products requiring steel include wind farms, greener buildings, zero emission vehicles, 'Jet Zero', green ships, green public transport, cycling, low-carbon hydrogen, advanced nuclear as well as carbon capture and storage. To illustrate future demand, it should be remembered that every 3.5MW wind-turbine installation used in the Rampion Windfarm required 1,200 tonnes of steel. If, as is estimated, 30GW of new capacity will be required this decade, produces demand in excess of 1 million tonnes of steel for offshore by 2030.

What does the UK steel industry look like today?

The UK steel industry employs ~70K people and delivers ~1.5 bn£ value add, yet enables a downstream with multiple of that size

2019

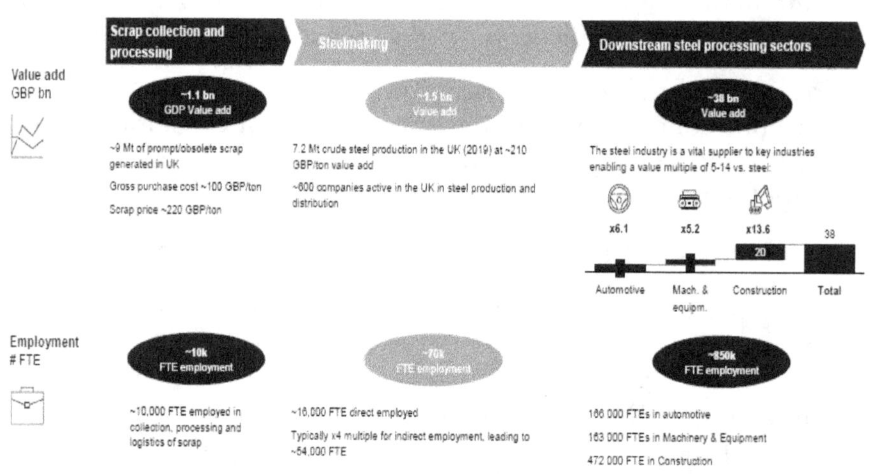

Source: Source: Expert interviews, IHS, Oxford economics, MetalBulletin, Press Search, ONS (24.1, 24.2, 24.3), EuroStat, Eurofer

The top 20 economies of the world benefit from indigenous steel industry. This sector is the bedrock of local supply-chain efficiency and facilitates the development of advanced manufacturing techniques and 'downstream' digital integration. However, in the UK, steel production has suffered substantial decline in both output and investment. Peak steel production in the UK of 28 million tonnes was achieved in 1970.

Currently it is a quarter of that at 7 million tonnes per year. Until 2000, the UK was a net exporter of steel but now imports over half of annual requirements.

It may be asked why has this happened? A UK corporate culture based on dividend rather than investment mitigates against asset heavy industries and does not help.

In the UK there is an investment and infrastructure environment which imposes penalties on energy, particularly electricity and combined with addon taxes such as business rates creates a competitive disadvantage which allows other nations to sell its product cheaper. This is particularly acute in the case of China where steel making is supported by the state.

Currently, more than half of all global production of steel occurs in China. Growth in China's steel making has been targeted at the European market. With repeated examples of questionable, some suggest, unfair trade practices, it's clear the growth of China's exports has severely undermined the competitiveness of many other nations including the UK.

Many countries have enacted unilateral trade defence mechanisms, most notably the USA (Section 232) whose steel making sector has suffered in a way similar to UK's in the past 20 years.

The UK has, in contrast to the USA, participated alongside or within the EU using, since 2018 and continuing until June 2021, safeguards on imports of certain steel products.

Unlike the US approach using Section 232, the EU implemented defences in respect of dumping as opposed to Section 232 which discriminates against steel for being made outside the US.

The EU / UK anti-dumping approach increasingly means that carbon taxes in Europe deepen the competitive disadvantage.

When anti-dumping legislation is applied to block unfair imports of steel – it is only applied if steel is dumped below cost and without carbon taxes, steel from China enjoys a cost advantage of £60 per tonne.

Effectively the current EU carbon taxation method ends up subsidising Chinese steel and steel intensive goods that contribute no carbon tax and reduce the production of cleaner / tax paying steel and manufacturing in UK and Europe.

National economic and steel make ranking 2018

Country	Crude Steel	Global ranking		
	(million tonnes)	GDP	Manufacturing	Steel
China	928	2	1	1
India	109	7	6	2
Japan	104	3	3	3
United States	87	1	2	4
Russia	72	13	15	6
Germany	42	4	4	7
Poland	10	25	24	19
Belgium	8	27	33	20
Egypt	8	47	44	21
UK	7	5	9	22
Austria	7	30	30	23
South Africa	6	36	42	26
Argentina	5	28	27	31
Qatar	3	56	63	40
Belarus	2.5	82		41

Source: **Total production of crude steel (worldsteel.org)**

The demand for steel or steel intensive goods in the UK (240 kilos of steel per year per person) is not an unusual consumption for a developed economy. The point of differentiation is how little of the steel consumed is produced in the UK.

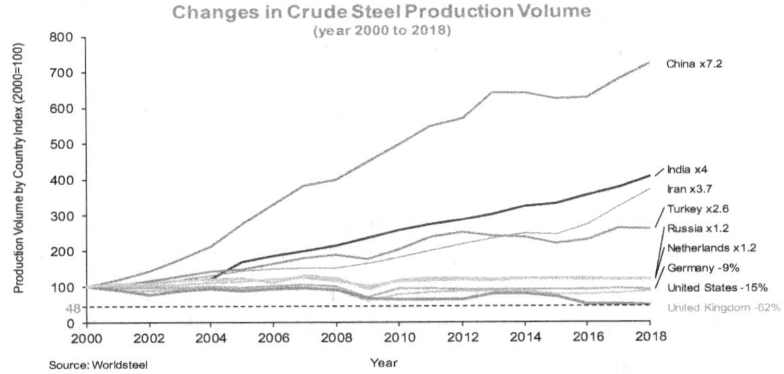

Source: **Total production of crude steel (worldsteel.org)**

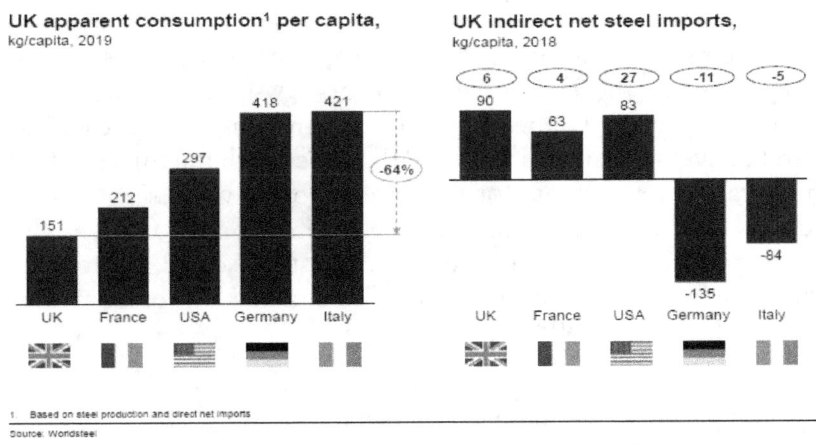

Source: **Apparent steel use (finished steel products) (worldsteel.org)**

What effects does this create?

Firstly, it constrains the knowledge economy for future manufacturing innovation and wealth creation. This damages future GDP-earning opportunities for the UK. Secondly it reduces the proportion of high value manufacturing elements of the economy reducing GDP and means considerably fewer high-skilled, well-paid jobs in the UK. Thirdly, it effectively exports carbon emission from this country to countries in which there is much less focus on carbon reduction.

Additionally, shipping of steel, a major source of pollution, adds to carbon emission. As a planet this is not good.

The steel industry is critical to the production element of the economy not simply for feedstock but also because of its impact on the knowledge economy. High strength steels have been critical to the development of electric vehicles ensuring the protection of occupants and the batteries. Cooperation is vital as shown by the collaboration between Tata Steel in Port Talbot and Warwick Automotive centre with Nissan to produce the original Nissan Leaf. Metallurgists and material scientists in the knowledge economy to support supply-chains will be even more critical during periods of substantive change such as the period of transition to zero carbon.

As the market for electric vehicles (EV) matures, we'll likely witness production facilities for Gigafactories being built with steel from the UK but high value steels for batteries being imported. Worse still for the electric motors and other high value components, we see few plant making these in the UK and to date no EV motor plant. To build wealth, not only do we need primary steelmaking in the UK, but the research, development and the GDP that goes with the full supply chain of high value components for the green economy. As seen below, the Industrial Manufacturing and Automotive sectors provide far higher contribution to GDP than the primary steel sector. Compared to Germany where this sector is worth 24.3% of GVA (the UK at 14.4%), it is possible to see GDP 'leakage'.

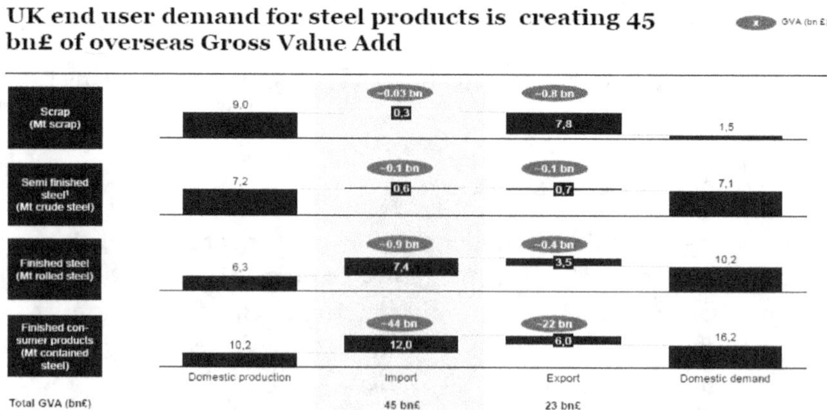

Source: WorldSteel, **Apparent steel use per capita (finished steel products) (worldsteel.org)**

Eurofer, SBB, Oxford economics

The UK's territorial emissions in relation to steel are 11.7 MT. This is directly as a consequence of production of the steel. However, consumption of steel, both direct and net imports of steel containing goods, give rise to an estimated 30 MT. Current reliance on steel imports leads to higher emissions if imported steel is produced at carbon-intensive steel plants. Global carbon intensity varies from 0.29-3.38 *tonnes of CO2 per tonne of crude steel* (tCO2/tcs), with the weighted average being 1.85tCO2/tcs.

At around 1.6tCO2/tonne of steel, UK steel production sites are much less carbon-intensive than the global average. This takes account of both blast furnace and electric arc furnace steelmaking. However, increased reliance on importation of steel will likely result in an increase in global CO2 emissions. Additionally, increased imports of finished steel products will also increase transport-related emissions. Shipping a tonne of product from China to the UK, results in an estimated 0.3 tonnes of additional CO2.

Solutions

There are a number of areas which require intervention and innovation: Energy; Investment Climate; Consumption-based accounting of emissions; Trade instruments; Public procurement.

Energy

The speed of transition to making all transport by EV as well as every home to use heat pumps are pertinent. There is the question of capacity of electricity to cope possibly leading to compromise. Green energy, essential to energy intensive industries such as steel making, will determine future competitiveness. It's therefore critical the transition from gas to hydrogen, or bridging biofuel options, takes place quickly to mitigate overdependence on electricity. Another challenge for electricity generators is to buffer mismatches between oversupply due to weather, i.e. wind power, and reduced seasonal demand. This may mean domestic battery, hydro storage and hydrogen generation.

Investment Climate

Government policy is a critical factor in determining attractiveness to private capital. The stock market relies on stable government policies over 20 to 30 years supporting investment whether through shareholders or banks. Appreciating the circumstances are benign to securing a greener UK steel industry is vital in underpinning the transition to net zero. This will include energy policy and the cost of energy. Electricity prices should, based on cleaner and renewable energy, become competitive based on government-backed power purchase agreements (similar to the nuclear programme long term electricity sale agreements).

Consumption-based accounting of emissions

There needs to be recognition of the fact that importing steel, as the UK largely engages in, does not recognise the impact on global emissions. Under current reporting norms based on the UK's Climate Change Act, such emissions are not considered. As such, achieving climate targets is possible through de-industrialisation rather than investment and innovation. Instead, the ambition of both government and industry should be to increase and decarbonise steel production in the UK. This would control consumption related emissions and protect as well as potentially create thousands of jobs.

Trade instruments

Trade instruments/carbon tax regimes would penalise polluting steel and steel intensive goods and allow green steel investments to benefit through return based on a 'level playing field'. It would incentivise innovation in steel needed as part of the transition to a green economy. This system would need to operate in conjunction with other nations, perhaps regionally with Europe adopting carbon border taxes while running consistent carbon tax and credit regimes to penalise internally polluters and incentivise green production. Such a regime would accelerate responsible change in Europe and incentivise other regions to adopt lower emissions thus saving the planet rather than closing European manufacturing and undermining innovation and employment it provides.

Public procurement

The UK Government should harness the buying power of its procurement departments to incentivise the use in public projects of low-CO2 steel. This will entail a product environmental policy which provides incentivises to manufacturers. There is also a need to establish strict eco-criteria for all imported products which would include carbon intensity of production as well as stipulations on durability, efficiency of energy performance whilst in use, as well as flexibility and ease of recovery at end of life consistent with the aspirations of developing a more circular economy. Ultimately, the public have shown their willingness to support energy efficiency schemes provided they are confident in their integrity.

Conclusion

Developing a green economy will not be achieved by closing manufacturing. The transition to green production requires considerable effort by dedicated manufacturers, discerning consumers and an environment, facilitated by government, which stimulates low carbon manufacturing and recycling. The legacy of the green revolution should be a UK which becomes an exemplar of being the 'green workshop' of the world.

About the Author

Tor Farquhar was the Executive Director of HR and IT for Tata Steel in Europe. Tor has worked in oil and gas, construction and steel and has sought to transform and modernise the foundation industries of economies across Asia Pacific and for the last 20 years Europe. A passionate advocate of modern manufacturing, whether through digital transformation, operational excellence, or agile ways of working, Tor works to design and deliver businesses that are more competitive through achieving sustainability economically, environmentally and societally.

Chapter Eleven

How the UK manufacturing sector can grasp the opportunities of new technologies and contribute to future sustainability

David Seall, Independent Director, Advisor and Chartered Engineer

Overview

This chapter details some of the challenges that the manufacturing sector within the United Kingdom currently face and how by embracing 'Industry 4.0', along with other exciting technologies, can create a truly circular economy.

Introduction

The greening of the United Kingdom's manufacturing economy has been underway for at least the last 25 years. It began with the push to outsource labour and energy intensive manufacturing processes to Central and Eastern Europe and China and the Far East at the end of the twentieth century. Large corporations sought to benefit from cheaper products and wanted reduced labour costs and were keen to build relationships with these growing economies to create new markets for their goods. They also wanted to reduce exposure to taxation, such as the poorly focussed Climate Change Levy in the UK and remain globally competitive.

Global Supply Chain Challenges

The carbon footprint of the UK reduced significantly and even the recycling of our waste was outsourced. However, our imported carbon footprint rose in proportion and thus the UK failed to reduce the true effect of our activities. The unprecedented economic disruption caused by COVID-19, uncertainty surrounding Brexit and the growing realisation of the catastrophic effects of climate change, have accelerated the need for the UK to revisit and change the way we consume and also produce the goods that we need to become globally competitive and create essential resilience in our economy.

These disruptions have emphasised that global, highly stretched, long distance supply chains have struggled to demonstrate resilience and even cross-channel supplies can no longer be guaranteed. Supplies of pharmaceuticals, medical equipment and food are now seen as vulnerable and the manufacturers of these are seen as strategically essential industries that should be based in the UK. Hence the increasing demand for re-shoring and the domestic production of critical products and services. This will inevitably lead to the potential for our own greenhouse emissions to rise with the increasing productive activity.

To mitigate this, it will not be adequate to go back to the old ways of production. Manufacturing industry needs to grasp the opportunities of using new energy sources, improved processes and less intensive consumption of resources. The impact of Industry 4.0 (which has been defined and explained in a multitude of sources), cannot be underestimated within this more strategic approach. The impact will be demonstrated in a number of key areas.

Supply Chain

It has been found that the supply chain contributes a significant contribution to an Original Equipment Manufacturers' (OEM) total carbon footprint. One global pharmaceutical manufacturer recently claimed that nearly 25 per cent of its carbon footprint was produced by the activities within its supply chain. The Industry 4.0 requirement for the digitally automated management of suppliers by the OEMs can lead to a more resilient and efficient system. The just-in-time production and delivery of components and parts will be finely honed and efficient. Over production and inventory will be minimised and the sources of production will be disaggregated from the current single sources and will be located closer to the point of demand. This will reduce the distances of parts travelled and make the shipping of container loads of 'stuff' less desirable. This reduction in transportation can also significantly reduce the carbon footprint of the products.

Additive manufacturing

Localised production can be made even more efficient by the use of additive manufacturing otherwise known as 3d printing. This is very 'pull focussed', whereby set up times and specific tooling requirements are minimised and only the parts needed at the time need to be produced. The only inventory required is the raw material whether metallic or polymer-based and this can be used across a range of parts. Additionally, parts produced tend to be more structurally efficient and consequently are lighter too. Porsche has recently developed an electric transmission casing additively manufactured in aluminium that is ten per cent lighter than the previous conventionally cast component. This technology enables these parts to be made near the point of use without the transportation and storage of finished parts. In theory these parts or parts like them could be produced at service and support centres. A case in point is that of Mercedes Benz which has already introduced 3d printers to print polymer parts in some its truck support centres in the USA.

Servitization

Another aspect of Industry 4.0 that will have a significant impact on the efficient use of resources is the advent of servitization. This is where the manufacturing company is not only responsible for the manufacturing of the part or assembly it is also responsible for the full support of the product through the entire service life of that product with the customer. We see this manifested at the moment with the Rolls Royce Aero engine model where airlines no longer buy engines but buy a service for the delivery of power from Rolls Royce, sometimes on an hourly basis. Rolls Royce maintain those engines and ensure optimum performance being rewarded with a long-term income stream for a fixed time period.

Those that buy their mobile phone service through a contract get a similar sort of service. Increasing responsibilities are placed on the supply chain to be both capable of providing in-service support but also to look at careful through life cost management. This means that reducing costs during manufacture, at the expense of longevity, is not in their best interests. An example of this would be the bus companies, who instead of buying the cheapest tyres for their fleet, move toward a service contract based on mileage of their buses. This drives the contractor to purchase the best tyres that not only have a longer initial life but because of superior carcass construction, these tyres can be re-treaded or "re-manufactured" two or three times. This reduces the overall environmental impact by reducing energy consumed and ensuring that materials remain in use and do not contaminate the environment.

This servitization model will move from B2B to B2C. Customers will use Internet of Things connected devices such as phones, TVs, domestic goods and cars and pay for the service - either via a pay as you go or by subscription. These products will know when to be serviced and will call out for the delivery and fitting of replacement parts. An autonomous vehicle may even drive itself to the service depot for overnight repair. Servitization also drives designers to create less modular designs which are then easier to repair in service. The adoption of 'right to repair' legislation across Europe encourages manufactures of consumer goods to build in repairability and reduce the modular, hard to replace and thus expensive nature of the componentry. Again, as we move from an ownership model to one of hire or rental, the onus moves to the supplier of goods to think long term about the relationship and support of the customer. It could be that the customer has a broom that has served them well for ten years but has had five handles and ten heads constantly maintained by the supplier!

Materials optimisation- Technology, Recycling and Remanufacturing

All of this means that the utilisation of materials is optimised, waste is not produced, either during the manufacturing process or at the end of life of the product as there is much reduced need for landfill. Alongside this is the search for more sustainable materials that require less energy to produce and also have less reliance of fossil fuels and other natural resources. Plastics sourced from organic sources such as sustainable sugar cane can be used. There have been significant moves to create more sustainably sourced composite materials using organic resins and natural fibres. For example, this has been regulated in some forms of motorsport for non-critical structural components thus avoiding the need for carbon fibres and epoxy-based resin systems.

These materials are less harmful for the environment at end of use. Even with conventional epoxy/carbon composites, waste materials and recycled parts are being remanufactured into other products, an example being carpet tiles for future Boeing aircraft. It has been said that a tonne of mobile phones contains more gold than 100 tonnes of ore. Recycling and remanufacturing will create a circular economy which will optimise the use of all materials, especially those that are expensive and strategically difficult to source and ensure that they remain in use without damaging our environment through disposal.

Energy

Underpinning the greening of manufacturing within the UK has to be the efficient use of energy and the use of renewables. The full electrification of industry needs to be incentivised and we must move quickly. Removing gas from the equation particularly when used for heating and especially ovens, needs to be addressed, perhaps by hydrogen conversion. With gas 25 per cent cheaper than electricity it's difficult to create a business case within an SME to change. In fact, this will be exacerbated when global demand reduces for fossil fuels at the end of the decade, when oil prices are predicted to drop to $20 a barrel. Economically viable and sustainable methods of producing and distributing hydrogen as an alternative fuel will need to be determined. Also, factories creating their own energy though solar panels and perhaps small wind turbines will only be viable if that energy can be stored and used within the factory. Cost efficient technology such as cheaper, heavier sodium batteries or even mechanical flywheel-based technologies may be the answer.

Skills

All of this new technology such as digitisation, servitization, supply chain management, new materials and green energy needs an upskilled workforce to enable this step forward. Manufacturing is in a competitive environment to capture these skills as they are in demand from many other sectors such as finance, business services and retail. A revitalised manufacturing sector needs to be able to train and secure this talent.

Conclusion

There is also a massive strategic gap in capabilities and awareness between the OEMs, at the top of the supply chains and the small and medium sized enterprises (SMEs) at the bottom. The OEMs, driven by their Boards and shareholders to address the issues of Environment, Sustainability and Governance (ESG) are funded and mandated to tackle these issues head on. Whilst the supply chain SMEs, which constitute a significant percentage of the total environmental footprint of an OEM, struggle to find the funds, skills and even management time to address these issues. Greater support to SMEs is going to be required to address the issue, especially as more of the supply chain will now be UK based.

Support with skills, advice, technology and especially intelligent procurement and funding will help. We will also need careful guiding of the energy market to encourage further electrification and the roll out of hydrogen for both combustion and use in fuel cells. Underpinning this is a strategic approach from Government that can create the climate for success. This involves addressing the key skills shortages, encouraging the use of more sustainable materials and most importantly determining a strategy for future industrialisation which creates resilience with export potential that has sustainability at the core.

About the author

David Seall CEng, FRAeS, MiMMM, FIoD, is a Fellow of both the Royal Aeronautical Society and the IoD. He is also a Member of IoM3 and a Freeman of the City of London. He is a Visiting Professor and Chair of the Advisory Board at the University of Surrey Business School and is a Member of the Manufacturing Commission advising the All-Party Parliamentary Manufacturing Group. He has been Regional Chairman of the IoD for the South of England and a Member of IoD Council. Previously he was Chief Executive of EEF South, now Make UK, working with hundreds of technology-based companies. Before this,

David had a long career in the aerospace industry working on major aircraft programmes for Boeing, Airbus and Eurofighter amongst others. He is a Member of the National Economic Policy Committee of Make UK. David has been a Non-Executive Director for over 20 years in both manufacturing and service companies as well as advising several start-up businesses, major banks and law firms. He has served as a Trustee for charities in the arts, education and mental health sectors.

Chapter Twelve

What can we learn from a 2-year, £1mn Innovate UK 'Advanced Methods of Construction' housing project?

Richard Haynes, Innovation and design consultant, working for Kiondo CIC, Associate Project Manager with Redmoor Health Ltd, Paul Nicol, Director of Advanced Methods of Construction, Hadley Group, Franco Cheung, Associate Professor, Birmingham City University

Overview

The chapter examines the multiple technological solutions available to those developing sustainable housing. As described, it's only through a shift in culture and a collaborative response that solutions to housing will be provided in an environmentally sustainable way. Crucially, some very practical lessons can be learnt and applied based on the case study that has been carried out by whg Housing based in the West Midlands.

Introduction

In 2019, whg Housing, a social housing landlord, was awarded a £972k Innovate UK grant to conduct a 2-year research and development project to pilot and prototype advanced methods of construction (AMC). This included developing a new platform-based Design for Manufacture and Assembly (DfMA) home and a Knowledge Based Engineering (KBE) tool (UK Research and Innovation, 2021). The primary objective was for whg to study how AMC may be applied to increase availability of affordable and environmentally sustainable homes. AMC as an approach to building homes has similarity to aerospace and automotive sector practices. This chapter focuses on the key principles, lessons learned during this case study and, crucially, the good practice which may be applied elsewhere.

The Project

The project was carried out by a consortium comprising whg (as lead), Birmingham City University, Energy Systems Catapult, Northmill Associates, Hadley Group and QM Systems. Other contributors were Savills, Walsall Council, NHBC, West Midlands Combined Authority, BRE and Manufacturing Technology Centre (MTC). In addition to the development of a new AMC approach, the consortium also attempted to address barriers such as access to finance by buyers, how mortgages built using entirely new construction methods might be secured, the lengthy planning process, relevant regulations for building materials, design standards, and affordability.

Key goals for homes to be delivered using the new approach included: providing healthier homes taking into account the well-being of residents; enabling design options using Advanced Methods of Construction (AMC); engaging industry leading manufacturers and suppliers; unlocking the redevelopment potential of brownfield land and improving neighbourhoods through housing development (e.g. redeveloping garage sites that are around maisonettes, low and high-rise flats where the garages are no longer fit for use with modern sized cars, and can attract crime and foster anti-social behaviours). Furthermore, the new approach was aimed at being adopted by projects in the pipeline of social housing development for Homes England and the West Midlands Combined Authority.

Brownfield Site

Existing garage site

Proposed new site

Principles

whg had a plan to build more than 350 new homes over a 2-year programme from over 200 sites identified across the West Midlands. AMC homes should be built as an alternative to traditional approaches due to space, planning and commercial limitations. Some key principles underpinning these developments were formulated at the outset and updated throughout the research project.

Modular inside and outside

The consortium wanted a scalable, flexible, design solution with modular units manufactured offsite in a factory environment using production line methods. A platform based DfMA house is intended to optimise prefabrication through increased automation and benefits of off-site construction though allowing sufficient customisation. Flexibility is factored in, so feasible design configurations can incorporate 'needs' and 'wants' of various clients as well as site requirements. Modular design can be adopted for both open and separate kitchen design. Modular house design can be delivered using an onsite panellised system, based on assembling housing units using building panels, volumetric systems, assembling housing units using 3 dimensional fully finished and installed pod units, or hybrid systems which are a combination of panellised and volumetric systems. In additional to 2-storey dwellings proposed in the project, the consortium developed a further design prototype for bungalows. The platform can be also extended for multi-storey housing design.

Design for high performance and low impacts. The AMC homes are designed in a holistic manner to ensure they include low impacts and high performance by reducing fuel poverty and energy consumption. The design criteria include:

(i) Adoption of renewable systems and (ii) Meeting target U-values for building elements.

Addressing the criteria will provide clean green energy and lower CO_2 emissions. AMC homes are equipped with smart technology delivering high-energy performance, low maintenance, running costs and energy bills.

Increasing Pre-Manufactured Value (PMV)

Government encourages adoption of AMC to improve productivity, health and safety on site, as well as deskilling on-site labour requirement, helping to make the industry more resilient to labour and skill shortages. PMV is a calculation of the amount of work carried out offsite in a building project. With the volumetric solution, AMC homes can increase PMV from less than 10% for traditional onsite construction to around 50%.

Ignoring Received Wisdom

Assumptions, traditional practices and existing wisdom have been questioned throughout the project. For example, lights were placed in the ceiling to avoid dangerous gas-pipes and ensure these were kept away from residents. Of course, though gas powered lighting is no longer fitted, the positioning of lighting remains unchanged. In older houses, lights are positioned close to the window. The team questioned whether artificial light might not mirror natural lighting more closely by rising from the floor, getting higher during the day, then lower as the sun is setting to better support circadian biological rhythms and supporting work, sleep and rest whilst simultaneously lowering usage and bills.

Likewise, electrical lights and power sockets have used alternating current since the mid 1880's (50 hz 230 volt). The whg AMC home incorporated ELE (extreme low energy) technology. This allows power distributed by CAT 6 data cabling rather than traditional electrical wiring meaning smart usage can be incorporated.

Image: https://www.insidehousing.co.uk/sponsored/sponsored/what-can-mmc-do-for-the-housing-crisis

Pragmatic, Human, Not Technology-led

Corner cupboards, not generally easy to access, became part of an adjacent 'plant room' (via the shared wall), making access for maintenance easier without losing space. Equipment and technology hardware upgrades could be achieved more simply. A prototype to test building methods and techniques was carried out to assess all aspects of home use and living patterns. The platform-based Design for Manufacture and Assembly approach standardises production processes and streamlines assembly of houses. It allows the construction of homes that improve well-being for all stakeholders throughout the whole-lifecycle, including design, build, use and decommissioning, enabling reuse of used materials. User research was carried out in conjunction with other housing teams at whg and through direct contact with customers at community engagement events.

Busting myths

How can a house be made of anything other than bricks and mortar yet meeting the expectation of typical house customers? The design prototype that the consortium developed has a façade system that can accommodate a variety of finish choices including brick tiles, weatherboard and rendering, etc.

How might key issues around financing and mortgaging new methods of construction be best addressed? The consortium consulted the National House Building Council (NHBC), an established insurance and accreditation body, early on to help to tackle some of these known objections downstream and myths around ideas of modular homes being robust and of good enough quality.

What's Been Learned

Branding

Ensuring understanding of the product by users and consumers is essential. Raising awareness of the benefits of modular, especially living in an AMC home, was crucial. Based on modelling work with Energy Systems Catapult, the energy consumption and bills for the best standard of AMC homes are likely to be 70% of those for a traditionally built home and use 50% of carbon typically produced.

Cost and benefit

AMC explicitly recognises problems of traditional approaches including skills shortages. It is anticipated that AMC build costs, assuming greater scale and improved efficiency, will decrease, making it a highly feasible and economically attractive alternative. In addition, there is significant saving in delivery time. For instance, it takes 27 weeks to build a traditionally built house but for AMC volumetric build, it will take only 3-4 days to construct the building above ground. DfMA approached applied tends to minimise unanticipated cost increases, which is favourable for affordable housing as cost certainty is vital.

Data and performance

Through much improved thermal insulation, performance of energy and lighting appliances, the overall construction the performance of AMC homes far outstrips traditional or existing methods. Early modelling, in 2019, of the design indicated significant energy and consumption savings (Energy Systems Catapult).

By adopting a fabric first approach ultimately with an increased thermally efficient structures, MEP does not need to be over-engineered. The prototype of AMC homes was tested by the Built Environment Climate Change Innovations (BECCI) team of University of Wolverhampton, including air leak tests, measurement of the U-values of the walls, windows and roof. The aim of the tests were to verify that the design met 0.16 U-value, the requirement of the building regulation, the results indeed confirmed a much higher standard, e.g. the wall actually achieved 0.13 U-value.

Birmingham City University designed and developed a Knowledge-Based Engineering tool (KBE), to ensure the most efficient approaches can be used at every stage. The KBE demonstrated showed reductions in both build and life-cycle costs through standardised processes and components. There were significant reductions in design and construction time, and energy consumption, and carbon emissions experienced by homeowners, tenants and landlords.

This prototype, based on the KBE tool, indicated homes built using AMC may potentially provide the following benefits: minimum of a 33% reduction in life-cycle costs; 10% reductions in building costs; 50% reduction in design and construction time.

DfMA houses may allow: energy consumption to be reduced by at least 30%; carbon emissions reduced by up to 50%; energy bills reduced by as much as 70%.

This creates significant savings to homeowners and makes such homes more affordable and sustainable. In an age of increasing 'fuel poverty' this is significant (UK Department of Energy and Climate Change, 2010).

In addition to these benefits, automating the production of panel provides the potential to manufacture more than 24,000 panels annually in a factory, sufficient to produce > 600 DfMA houses.

Conclusion

By bringing together and integrating experts from various specialist sectors and by continuous improvement of the products and processes by identifying automation potentials using Knowledge-based Engineering (KBE) tools, the consortium together created a high output, mass customised, high quality high performing and low cost, low impact, housing offer. Access to critical performance data that is so close to the objectives we set for affordable housing providers such as whole lifecycle costs, embedded emissions and CO2 emissions in use, has never previously been available to the sector.

There were significant additional outcomes as a result of the work relating to certain deliverables. The prototype was instrumental in the success of this before the pandemic stopped further activity. Additionally, the KBE tool has been greatly enhanced through constant test and feedback to include additional financial data from WHG along with whole lifecycle cost data commissioned by WHG.

About the authors

Richard Haynes is an Innovation and design consultant, working for Kiondo CIC, a community led design agency and Associate Project Manager with Redmoor Health Ltd. Richard has extensive experience working across health, social care and housing and has reviewed and provided input for the CECOPS International Code of Practice for Technology Enabled Care. Richard possesses an MSc in Technology and his research interests lie in systems, and design thinking, where health, housing and social care issues intersect. He's is currently working with the RCA and Sheffield University on an Arts and Humanities Research Council funded project to better understand the built landscape and natural environment including the role nature-based solutions have in mental and physical health and well-being.

Paul Nicol is Director of AMC, Hadley Group. His roles at Hadley are to direct and lead on all AMC activities including creating the manufacturing facility for new modular products and a suite of offsite solutions for the industry. He has 25 years of construction and manufacturing experience and specialises in Project Management and Delivery Management, his particular expertise is with structural and facades. He has delivered a portfolio of construction projects for different clients ranging from £250k-£25M such as; housing projects (traditional and off-site), PFI Schools, MOJ Custodial off-site accommodation and Justice Centres. He has a keen interest in delivering modular housing that reduces the in-living cost by presenting renewables and technology as part of the integrated design, and exceeds the mandate for time, cost and quality of the industry.

Dr Franco Cheung, is Associate Professor at Birmingham City University. He specialises in the development and use of cost models. His research interests include off-site manufacturing, calculation of life-cycle costing, evaluation of the carbon footprint of a building, cost management, ontologies, and knowledge-based engineering. He led the Innovation UK funded project: Collaborative knowledge-based Design for Manufacture and Assembly (DfMA) approach to building cost-efficient, low-impact and high-performance houses, in which Hadley and BCU were key partners. Franco was the principal investigator, leading a multi-disciplinary BCU team comprising architectural modeller and computer scientist and software engineer in developing a proof-of-concept knowledge-based engineering tool for DfMA houses.

References

Edlira Vakaj Kalemi, Franco Cheung, Abdel-Rahman Tawil, Panagiotis Patlakas, Kudirat Alyana (2020) ifcOWL-DfMA a new ontology for the offsite construction domain, Proceedings of the 8th Linked Data in Architecture and Construction Workshop - LDAC2020

Kudirat Ayinla, Edlira Vakaj, Franco Cheung, and Abdel-Rahman H. Tawil (Accepted in 2021) A Semantic Offsite Construction Digital Twin- Offsite Manufacturing Production Workflow (OPW) Ontology, SeDiT 2021

References accessible online:

West Midlands DfMA: https://tc-catalogue.strongerstories.org/stories/west-midlands-dfma/

Hadley Group's Steel Framing Structure offers lightweight and efficient solution for Coventry Modular Housing Project: https://www.hadleygroup.com/case-studies/hadley-groups-steelframing-structure-offers-lightweight-and-efficient-solution-for-coventry-modular-housingproject

Transforming house construction with DfMA: https://www.bcu.ac.uk/builtenvironment/research/transforming-building-life-cycle/research-projects/transforminghouse-construction-using-design-for-manufacture-and-assembly

Platform design for manufacture and assembly of housing: https://www.bcu.ac.uk/builtenvironment/research/transforming-building-life-cycle/research-projects/platform-designfor-manufacture-and-assembly-of-housing

DfMA House Panel Production: https://www.bcu.ac.uk/built-environment/research/transforming-building-lifecycle/research-projects/dfma-house-panel-production

DfMA house knowledge-based engineering (KBE) tool for Life Cycle Cost and CO2 emissions: https://www.bcu.ac.uk/built-environment/research/transforming-building-lifecycle/research-projects/dfma-house-kbe-tool-for-life-cycle-cost-and-co2-emissions

Energy Modelling of Modular DfMA Housing for Walsall Housing Group: https://es.catapult.org.uk/reports/energy-modelling-of-modular-housing/

Chapter Thirteen

Biomethane, a Case Study based on Successful Circular Economy Practice

Beverley Nielsen, Executive Director and Associate Professor,
Institute of Design, Economic Acceleration & Sustainability (IDEAS),
Birmingham City University

*"We are wrecking our world - the one place we call home - risking
our health, security and survival here on Earth. Now nature is
sending us a desperate SOS and time is running out."*
Tanya Steele, chief executive at WWF (Briggs H, 2020)

Biomethane – the lesser-known green gas

As nature signals SOS with wildlife populations declining more than
two-thirds in 50 years, nature offers solutions too, for example by
harnessing the circular economy green gas and energy dense fuel,
biomethane, produced from naturally occurring organic waste
materials – food, crop, animal and human wastes. Drawing on
biomethane, we can prevent harmful methane emissions – 34 times
more harmful than carbon dioxide (IPPC, 2013) - identified by the UN
Environment programme as responsible for around 30% of warming
since the pre-industrial era (UN News, 2021).

Biomethane and fossil natural gas (CNG) are chemically identical with
biomethane (Bio-CNG) currently injected to grid through buying and
selling renewable gas, evidenced by certificates and mass balancing
(similar to that for green electricity). This green gas is already available
and companies such as Severn Trent plc are injecting biomethane to
grid providing energy capable of heating 22,000 homes. With the
country focussed on converting much of the overall gas network to
hydrogen, biomethane can provide an immediate pathway to lower
greenhouse gas (GHG) emissions for gas companies looking to reach
targets, including saving an estimated 40 million tonnes of CO2
emissions every year (ENA, 2020).

Already available for use in transport, biomethane is especially
practical as an alternative for heavier vehicles – HGVs, trains, trams,

buses, refuse trucks – whilst also available for use in heating and energy generation. One kilogram of biomethane is capable of providing the energy output associated with well over one litre of both diesel and petrol. Mandatory food waste collection will provide an opportunity to increase biomethane production and use whilst eliminating this waste stream to landfill (Defra February 2020).

Preventing Methane emissions

Earlier in May 2021, Inger Andersen, UN Under Secretary-General and Executive Director for the United Nations Environment Programme (UNEP) stated, "Cutting methane is the strongest lever we have to slow climate change over the next 25 years and complements necessary efforts to reduce carbon dioxide. The benefits to society, economies, and the environment are numerous and far outweigh the cost." (UN News, 2021).

The UNEP Report, Global Methane Assessment, (UNEP 2021) highlighted that cutting human-caused methane emissions by 45% this decade would keep warming beneath a threshold agreed by world leaders. Reducing human-caused methane emissions was highlighted as one of the most cost-effective strategies to rapidly reducing the rate of warming and contributing significantly to global efforts to limit temperature rise to 1.5°C. This would avoid nearly 0.3°C of global warming by the 2040s whilst complementing all long-term climate change mitigation efforts. It would also prevent, on an annual basis, 255,000 premature deaths, 775,000 asthma related hospital visits, 73 billion hours of lost labour from extreme heat, and 26 million tonnes of crop losses globally.

The Birmingham Biomethane Cluster

The *Birmingham Biomethane Cluster*, launched by the *IDEAS* in 2020, has brought together companies engaged in biomethane production, distribution and use, regionally, across the UK and internationally, with a focus on *capturing* methane emissions to harness this valuable energy source whilst also cutting these potentially harmful emissions as advocated by UNEP (Ravishankara *et al.*, 2021). The group has provided greater clarity around the strength and depth of expertise in the West Midlands, the investable opportunities and highlighted the role already played by individual companies in the region.

Case Study: Severn Trent Water and Severn Trent Green Power

Severn Trent Water handles the regulated business of supplying water and recycling human waste safely, whilst subsidiary company, Severn Trent Green Power, was established to set up and run anaerobic digestion (AD) facilities running on food and crop waste.

Severn Trent Bioresources runs 27 AD sites servicing 1008 sewage treatment works and has been developing anaerobic digestion treatment of the waste from 8.1m people in the Midlands to recover two very valuable materials – Biosolids which return nutrients to farmland and Biogas for renewable energy production.

In February 2020 Severn Trent plc announced their 2030 Triple Carbon Pledge to deliver: 100% of their energy sourced from renewable generation; Net Zero Carbon emissions; 100% Electrical fleet (where technology allows).

Having already met the first challenge, this business envisages a very substantial role for biomethane production and use in assisting them reach their remaining targets – as a power generator, heat generator and a vehicle fuel.

Severn Trent Water currently produces just under 600 gigawatt hours (GWh) per annum of biogas from anaerobic digestion, with 118 GWh of this converted into biomethane and injected into the grid (the remainder being used for CHP generation at their own sites). This amount of biomethane provides the equivalent power required for heating approximately 10,000 homes or continuously powering 240 HGVs. If Severn Trent Water converted all of its biogas into biomethane, they could heat approximately 50,000 homes or power around 1,200 HGVs. The current combined biomethane produced by both Severn Trent Water and Severn Trent Green Power and injected to grid could heat 22,000 homes or power over 500 HGVs, highlighting the value of this little harnessed green gas and energy source.

Severn Trent's treatment plant at Minworth services just over 2m people, producing 1400 normal meter cubes per hour (nmch) of biomethane. Commissioned in 2014, this was the first commercial sewage to biomethane plant in the UK. It was also the first to inject biomethane into the national gas grid working with Cadent Gas.

A water scrubbing system was selected to produce biomethane appropriate for injection to grid at Minworth and chosen as a well-established technology widely used throughout Europe with a low heating requirement and a 97% methane recovery potential.

The Finham sewage treatment works in Coventry processes waste from 1m households. First commissioned in early 2021, it produces 1500 nmch of Biomethane and represents Severn Trent Water's fourth sewage to biomethane production plant injecting gas to grid and drawing on a membrane upgrading system as a proven technology in use in the UK since 2016.

This method of biomethane production has the advantage of a higher methane recovery rate at 99%+ with the potential for CO2 recovery, not possible through water scrubbing systems.

Like other companies operating HGV fleets on biomethane, including Waitrose, John Lewis, Hermes and most recently, Royal Mail, Severn Trent Water are also trialling biomethane to power their fleet of 90 tankers in seeking to reach 2030 corporate targets. The company is aware of a continuing role for steam reformation of methane in the production of Hydrogen.

However rather than using fossil fuel methane, currently used in the production of around 96% of all hydrogen in use worldwide, their ambitions include using renewable biomethane as a basis for hydrogen production.

Severn Trent Water is currently developing three new Advanced Anaerobic Digestion (AAD) sites, combining these with new biomethane plants to join the existing biomethane production in Birmingham and Stoke on Trent. Two of these sites have construction underway, with their gas to grid plant already on stream.

They are also planning to commission a plant using CO2 from the biomethane upgrader, or a CHP exhaust, to produce a pelletized fertilizer product.

Severn Trent Water wastewater anaerobic digestion process (courtesy Severn Trent Water)

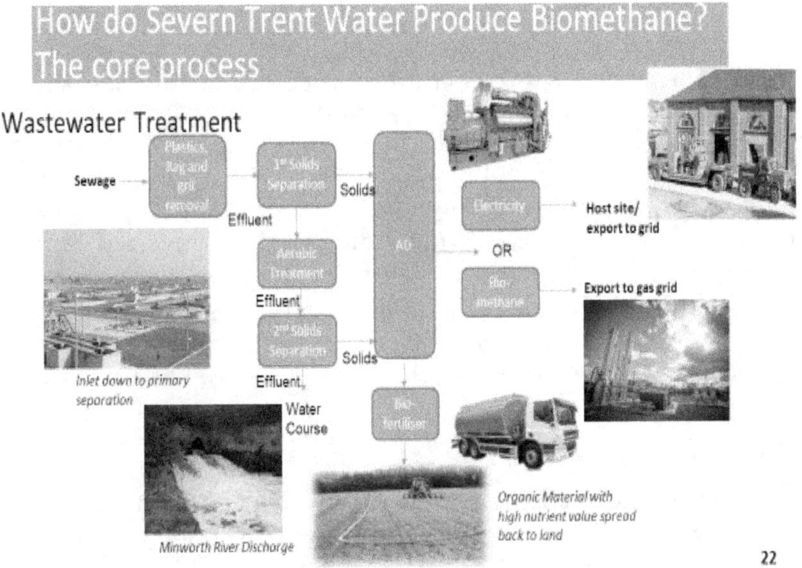

Set up as a subsidiary focused on renewable power development, Severn Trent Green Power acquired Agrivert in late 2018, a business already operating five food waste AD plants, as well as five compost plants, and which had previously contracted two food waste AD plants to Severn Trent Green Power.

Severn Trent Green Power now owns and operates seven plants in Oxfordshire, Berkshire, South Wales, North and West London and East and West Birmingham, with all its plants following the same design drawing on their proven track record.

An eighth plant is going through the final stages of commissioning in Derby.

Through these plants the company has capacity to process food waste from over 4 million households or 400,000 tonnes of food waste in total.

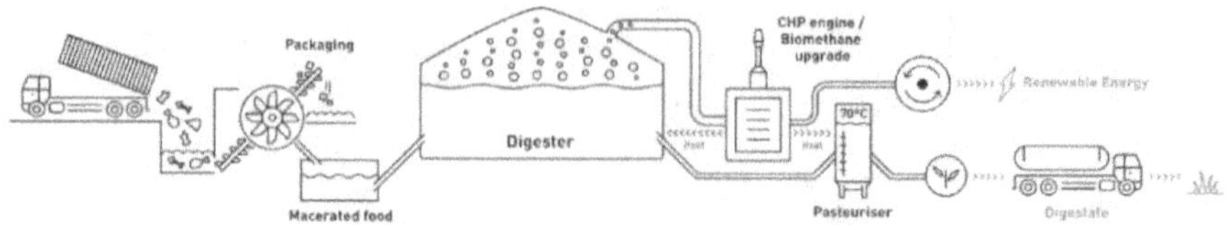

Food Waste Anaerobic Digestion process; courtesy Severn Trent Green Power

The process involves tipping food waste into a bunker, passing this through the 'mouth' enabling the separation of any packaging or contamination from the organic material and converted into a soup. The soup is fed, in turn, into one of five digesters with long retention times of around 90 days, helping to ensure stability, assisting gas extraction and improving quality of the resulting digestate. The biogas is fed either into a CHP to produce electricity or further processed to inject directly into the gas grid – either way producing renewable energy.

Over half of the feedstock input is from local authority household waste – with Severn Trent Green Power servicing over 50 local authorities or 25% of the country's household food waste. The remainder of Severn Trent Green Power's work applies to servicing food manufacturing, major trade waste collectors, many independents and large supermarkets, as well as the commercial sector. The business estimates that mandatory food waste collections, due from 2023, will yield sufficient food waste to power 20-30 additional AD plants across England.

Mandatory Food Waste Collection – the opportunity

A recent consultation by the Department for the Environment, Food Waste and Rural Affairs (Defra) indicated that if all local authorities provided kerbside food waste collection, the amount of food waste collected would increase by 1.35m tonnes by 2029 - reducing GHG emissions by around 1.25 million tonnes per year and preventing food waste to landfill (Defra, 2020). Mandatory food waste collections have since been planned as part of the Environment Bill, due to be passed into law second half 2021 (Speechlys, April 2021)

Food waste collection is already mandatory in Scotland and Wales. The Scottish government began rolling out food waste recycling to all households in 2011 leading to a drop in household food waste of 7% across Scotland since 2009 compared with a 4.2% rise in household waste from 2012 to 2015 across the UK as a whole. Just three years ago, FareShare branches in Scotland received 350 tonnes of surplus food from retailers and manufacturers, which increased by 443% to 1,900 tonnes in 2016. In 2017 volumes grew 43%, more than double the 19% growth across the rest of the UK. (Tatum M, April 2017)

Since mandatory food waste collections in Scotland a survey published in 2019 'Scottish anaerobic digestion and biogas sector survey 2017' showed that overall the AD sector in 2017 generated 217 million m3 of biogas, with significant growth in the industrial and farming sectors accounting for 68% of the total (Menzies, B, et al, March 2019). The survey showed food waste accounted for an overall total of 175,951 tonnes, compared with an overall total of 141,028 tonnes (composting and AD) processed in 2014.

Feedback from stakeholders engaged in the project pointed to other areas with the potential for significant development in the future. Firstly, the industrial sector had, it was felt, significant room for growth, with many thousands of tonnes of potential feedstock currently discharged to sea and/or land. Secondly, there was potential in terms of on-site AD at the smaller, more remote distilleries, dairy food processors, brewers etc. The energy value of food residues was not recognised by food companies and much greater effort was needed to highlight the opportunity. Thirdly, municipal waste collections, including households' participation levels, could be significantly improved. It was estimated that around 29% of residual household black bag waste consists of food waste, with over one million tonnes of household waste being landfilled in 2017. This indicated real potential for recovering significant food waste tonnages for anaerobic digestion/composting. Finally, increasing awareness-raising work was required to improve participation levels and reduce contamination such as through food packaging.

Biomethane: a sustainable solution for HGVs

In terms of sustainable fuel distribution, companies such as CNG Services Ltd (CSL) are providing consultancy, design and build services to the biomethane industry, focused on reducing greenhouse gas (GHG) emissions. In the past 10 years the efforts of this company alone have led to an estimated reduction in CO_2 emissions of 17,500,000 tonnes through the following: Biomethane injection to the gas grid; Running trucks on Bio-CNG; Acting as developer and design and build contractor for the Highlands Bio-CNG Project.

Modelled Well-to-Wheel (WTW) emissions for Bio-CNG trucks indicate at least 85% GHG emissions saving compared to diesel equivalents. For manure feedstock the GHG saving is over 100% because of avoided methane emissions.

Whilst many companies are already operating Bio-CNG vehicles – many others could still do so. For example, all construction could use cement mixers run on Bio-CNG as Iveco, Mercedes and Scania are all producing these vehicles. Some companies, such as Ultra-Light Rail Partners, are promoting biomethane-powered carbon neutral trams and trains as a pathway to harnessing hydrogen through compatible powertrains.

Image 1: St Chad's Metro Halt, Birmingham, without requirement for overhead power drawing on affordable, renewable biomethane-powered trams (image courtesy of Ultra-Light Rail Partners)

A national network of fuel depots, being developed by CNG Fuels and Foresight Group, including the Erdington depot in Birmingham, has ensured that all fuel depots are located conveniently close to the motorway network and is providing an immediate advantages enabling GHG savings at once without waiting for any new technology.

References

Briggs H, (2020), 'Wildlife in 'catastrophic decline' due to human destruction, scientists warn', *BBC* https://www.bbc.co.uk/news/science-environment-54091048, 10th September, accessed 15th May, 2021

ENA, (2020), 'Gas Goes Green, Britain's Hydrogen Network Plan', https://www.energynetworks.org/industry-hub/resource-library/britains-hydrogen-network-plan.pdf#:~:text=Green%20programme%2C%20Britain%E2%80%99s%20Hydrogen%20Network%20Plan%20will%20play,to%20be%20transported%20for%20use%20in%20different%20sectors, December, accessed 15th May 2021

Defra, (2020), 'Household food waste to be collected separately by 2023', Defra, https://deframedia.blog.gov.uk/2020/02/10/household-food-waste-to-be-collected-separately-by-2023-and-50000-city-trees-to-be-planted-in-urban-tree-challenge-fund/, 10th February accessed 15th May 2021

IPCC, (2013), *Climate Change 2013: The Physical Science Basis. Contribution of Working Group I to the Fifth Assessment Report of the Intergovernmental Panel on Climate Change*, edited by Stocker, T.F., Qin, D., Plattner, G.K, Tignor, M., Allen, S.K., Boschung, J., Nauels, A. Xia, Y., Bex, V. and Midgley, P.M., Cambridge University Press, Cambridge, UK

Menzies B, Dimambro M. and Aspray T. (2019) 'Scottish anaerobic digestion and biogas sector survey 2017, Zero Waste Scotland', https://www.zerowastescotland.org.uk/sites/default/files/Scottish%20anaerobic%20digestion%20and%20biogas%20sector%20survey%202017.pdf, 29th March, accessed 15th May 2021

Speechlys C.R. (2021), *Delayed Environment Bill To Return Autumn 2021*, *Lexology*, https://www.lexology.com/library/detail.aspx?g=c067d77a-c8ce-44ff-9383-4ce77306ece7, 20th April, accessed 15th May 2021

Tatum, M. (2017), How Scotland has Food Waste All Wrapped Up, *The Grocer*, https://www.thegrocer.co.uk/food-waste/how-scotland-has-food-waste-wrapped-up/551024.article, 10th April, accessed 15th May 2021

UN News, (2021), 'Cut methane emissions to avert global temperature rise, UN-backed study urges', UN, https://news.un.org/en/story/2021/05/1091402, **6th May,** accessed 15th May 2021

Ravishankara, A. R. , Kuylenstierna, J.C.I., Michalopoulou, E., HöglundIsaksson, L., Zhang, Y., Seltzer, K., Ru, M., Castelino, R., Faluvegi, G., Naik, V., Horowitz, L., He, J., Lamarque, J-F., Sudo, K., Collins, W.J., Malley, C., Harmsen, M., Stark, K., Junkin, J., Li, G., Glick, A., and Borgford-Parnell N. (2021), Global Methane Assessment, Summary for Decision Makers, United Nations Environmental Programme, Paris, France

Chapter Fourteen

Carbon Farming - A New and Profitable Crop for Farmers

Craig Sams, co-founder of Green & Black's, advocate of sustainable farming and founder of Carbon Gold

Overview

I was visiting a cousin in Iowa a few years ago and it was raining heavily all day at the end of July, just as the ears were ripening on the corn. In the early evening, he got a call from another farmer that corn was down a dollar a bushel - the traders in Chicago had seen the level of rain, calculated how much bigger the corn crop would be as a result and marked down the price by 20% accordingly. That has always been the case, supply and demand and sharp traders define prices. Now there's a new crop that will change the game for farmers for the first time in history - Carbon. Beautiful stuff - you harvest it out of 'thin' air and nobody can 'screw' you on the price.

Nobody wants to turn down the central heating in the winter or the air conditioning in summer or cancel their timeshare in Tenerife. Energy is very cheap and if it comes to the crunch, people will pay the carbon cost of these luxuries rather than give them up. With carbon pricing, they will just have to pay a bit more. So far, nobody has to pay for their carbon dioxide emissions. But we all pay in the end as we are generating a climate crisis that marks the end of civilisation as we know and love it.

Every time we emit carbon dioxide (CO_2), it eventually finds its way back to earth. If it didn't then there wouldn't be any plants or any food, as plants can't grow without carbon dioxide. So, it's not a bad thing. Carbon is the foundation of all life.

Then why the fuss about global warming? Let's consider some statistics. The carbon dioxide that we release comes from:

Fossil Fuels (energy, industry, transportation): 33 billion tonnes

Farming (livestock, fertiliser runoff, soil erosion): 10 billion tonnes

This gives a total annual emission of C02 of 43 billion tonnes.

Then land and ocean take 20 billion tonnes out of the atmosphere. That leaves an annual increase of 23 billion tonnes. That's the problem. How can we increase the amount that land and ocean take out? Soil, trees, hay and hemp can do the job. These are 'Nature-based Solutions.' They can remove way more than the 23 billion tonnes that we need to reduce, it's just a question of how we manage them.

Soil

Arable farmland alone is 1.5 billion hectares globally and 'carbon farming' can take out a lot. Soil is a great carbon 'sink' or storage space. La Vialla, a biodynamic farm near Florence, takes 13 tonnes of CO2 out of the atmosphere per hectare every year and locks it up in their fertile soil. This is validated every year by the University of Siena. La Vialla are very clever farmers so let's say the average farmer just takes 12 tonnes per hectare out, 12 x 1.5 billion is 18 billion tonnes of CO2 transformed from CO2 in the atmosphere to carbon-rich organic matter in the soil. So, soil alone can theoretically offset 18 billion tonnes of annual emissions. But that's not enough. We need trees, hemp and hay, too.

Trees

We chop millions of trees down every year and burn them in places like Drax Power Station. The smoke is toxic and causes lung disease, it's dirtier than coal. The trees grow in Arkansas and Louisiana and are pelleted and shipped across the Atlantic (big carbon footprint). It would be cleaner and less climate-damaging if we left the trees alone and burned coal or oil or gas. The Dutch burn palm oil in power stations. In the UK and the EU we mix it into biodiesel as motor fuel to comply with the EU Renewable Transport Fuels Obligation. Burning food has to stop and has a higher carbon footprint than burning fossil fuels.

$600 billion is given annually to farmers in the West in the form of subsidies. They grow sugar beet, corn, wheat, barley and wine that we turn into ethanol and mix into petrol. They grow rapeseed, oil palm and soybeans that mix into diesel. Just imagine if that money went to capturing carbon in their soils and increasing forest cover instead of killing the soil with chemical fertilisers to grow food crops for burning while at least 25,000 people a day die of hunger.

If we got it right we could soon be stressing about Global Cooling.

Global Cooling has happened before. There was the 'Little Ice Age.' It lasted for hundreds of years, right up until the early 1800s. In 1683 the River Thames froze over completely for 2 months with ice 11 inches thick and there were 'Frost Fairs' every winter. The Dutch happily skated up and down their frozen canals.

That happened because the Plague had reduced the world's population of farmers by 50%, followed by Spanish and English settlements of America which reduced the native populations by 90% from measles, colds and smallpox. As a result, there weren't nearly as many people as there had previously been on the planet. With so many humans dead and not farming, trees reclaimed their territory. The Amazon was full of rich farming communities, led by ferocious women (that's how it got its name). When the natives of North and South America died, the forests came back with a vengeance.

All those new trees in North and South America, Europe and Central Asia sucked huge amounts of carbon dioxide out of the atmosphere, leading to the Little Ice Age and Global Cooling. We were saved by the steam engine that helped us increase carbon dioxide in the atmosphere by burning coal. To help warm things further, Europe's population recovered and cut down forests to grow wheat and rye. Many Europeans went to farm in the Americas, cutting down forests there and ploughing up prairies, increasing, even more, the amount of carbon dioxide in the atmosphere. Until 1980, farming was responsible for half the annual increase in greenhouse gas levels. Since then it has increased its emissions, but not as fast as industry and transportation

That's how things warmed up. But now it's gone too far. We are overshooting. Time to twiddle the climate knobs and adjust our temperature downwards by reducing carbon dioxide from the atmosphere. If we could make it cold before, we can do it again, (ideally without the Plague and smallpox epidemics, of course).

What would we do with all the trees? Well one thing is just to leave them alone. Mature forests keep on pumping CO_2 out of the atmosphere and store it in the soil and in their wood. A lot of wood in buildings could replace steel and concrete, which will become more expensive with carbon pricing. Locking wood away in a building would get carbon offset income.

New technologies like 'Glulam,' a super hard form of plywood, mean that you can build skyscrapers out of wood. There is now a 20-storey student accommodation building in Vancouver made of wood. Sumitomo Forestry in Tokyo are building a 70 storey 'plyscraper' that will be able to flex with the next earthquake. I live in a house that was built of oak in 1770. The carbon in our floors and beams was carbon dioxide way back when William the Conqueror came ashore a few miles down the coast. Using wood instead of steel and concrete is win-win: less emissions and more sequestration. 5 billion hectares of the Earth are trees. Conservatively allow 4 tonnes per hectare per annum and you are up to 20 billion tonnes CO2 sequestered annually.

Hemp

In 1885 my great grandfather Ole Doxtad ploughed virgin prairie in Nebraska that had 100 tonnes of carbon per hectare. By the time I was born ploughing had reduced that to 10 tonnes, the rest went into the atmosphere. His son Lewis, my grandpa, patriotically grew hemp on our farm during World War 2. The US Navy needed it for rope and canvas, ('canvas' comes from 'cannabis'). It helped rebuild the soils on our farm.

After the war polypropylene replaced hemp rope and there was no market for hemp, which then became illegal to grow. But it spread everywhere and is known as 'ditchweed'. Because hemp crowds out all other weeds a crop rotation with hemp would eliminate carcinogenic weedkillers like 'Roundup,', reducing the incidence of cancer and 'Non-Hodgkin' lymphoma, a blood cancer that affects teenagers and young people. Nothing kills weeds like weed!

Nothing grows as fast as hemp, either. It can capture 22 tonnes of CO2 per hectare per year. If just one billion of our 4 billion hectares of pasture were planted with hemp that would be 22 billion tonnes of CO2 out of the atmosphere, every year. There would still be 3 billion hectares left of pasture for grazing. The leaves of the hemp plants would make good animal feed, along with the meal after the hemp seed oil is extracted.

There are 4 billion hectares of pasture globally. If farmers planted wildflower meadows they would still get a crop of hay once a year but there would also be 11 tonnes per hectare of CO2 sequestered deep in the ground by the roots of the grasses and flowers. But we already took 1 billion hectares for hemp. So that leaves 3 billion for hay. At 11 tonnes per hectare that's 33 billion tonnes of CO2. With a carbon price of £50, a hectare of wildflower hay meadow would earn a farmer £550 of carbon income, plus 6 tonnes of hay at £100 per tonne. That's more than they make from sheep or cows.

If farmers got paid for growing carbon and keeping it in the soil, they would farm with respect for nature, rebuild our degraded soils, increase biodiversity, increase woodland cover, and make our landscape more beautiful. We don't want to overshoot the target and we still need to grow food. The price of meat would go up with carbon pricing. People would eat more grains and vegetables and less processed food. We don't have to go vegan, but with 42% obesity rates in the US and 33% in the UK a little bit less food might not be a bad thing.

Biochar

Biochar is charcoal made for agricultural use. Biochar is 80% pure carbon, reflecting the high carbon content of the wood or biomass feedstock. Farmers and gardeners put it in the soil and it stays there for hundreds if not thousands of years. It encourages the positive biology that keeps plants healthy (it cures ash dieback and honey fungus), it holds onto nutrients that might otherwise wash away and it keeps soils from drying out. Biochar prevents soil compaction and is now being used widely to plant urban trees as it increases their survival rate. It is a great way to deal with wood waste. It is also an effective alternative to peat, which is being phased out by gardeners but still used by commercial growers. Making biochar from wood waste instead of burning it could generate another 5 billion tonnes a year of carbon offsets.

The Maths

Amount taken out by regenerative farming of soil: 18 billion tonnes

Amount taken out by hemp: 22 billion tonnes

Amount taken out by wildflower meadows: 33 billion tonnes

Amount taken out by not burning wood and growing trees: 20 billion tonnes

Biochar - 5 billion tonnes

Ocean sink - 10 billion tonnes

Total: 108 billion tonnes annually

Annual Greenhouse Gas emissions: 43 billion tonnes

Total taken out by farming, hemp, forests, meadows, ocean and biochar: 108 billion tonnes

Net annual reduction in atmospheric carbon dioxide: 43 bn - 108 bn = 65 billion tonnes CO2 reduction per year.

Conclusion

The CO2 level in 1850 was 285ppm. Every ppm is 17 billion tonnes. So in a perfect world we could take out at almost 4 ppm every year. To get back to the 1850 level would be 130 ÷ 4 = 32 years. With the same level of CO2 emissions from energy, industry and transport. Of course, many technologies such as solar and wind are already helping to reduce fossil fuel emissions.

We need to put a price on carbon, making the people who emit it pay the cost and pay that money to the farmers and builders who are locking it away, using nature-based solutions. A bonus would be cleaner air, more biodiversity, cleaner rivers and seas and happier farmers. This is beginning to happen and the end result will be the salvation of our beloved planet.

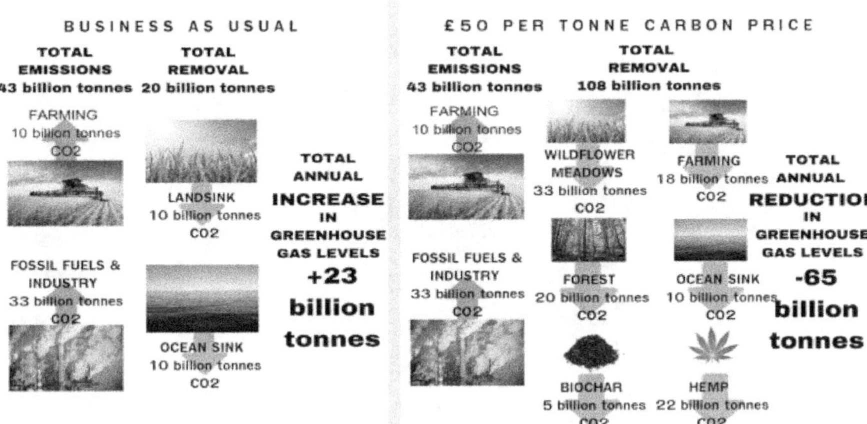

About the author

Craig Sams is a co-founder of Green & Black's and has inspired and provided leadership for #biochar revolution with Carbon Gold. Craig founded Carbon Gold in 2007 to campaign for reduction pollution in farming that is leading to climate change. Craig is a director of the Soil Association Certification Ltd and enthusiastically supports methods of using land that are less harmful to the environment.

Carbon Gold, a carbon sequestration business based on the use of biochar as a soil improver, supports sustainable food production through the development of biochar-based products and projects. Through his work with Carbon Gold as well as being a passionate advocate of change, Craig believes it is essential to support our natural ecosystems which will create opportunities for economic improvement that are more equitable and provide benefit to those engaged in agriculture.

Afterword

Jack Dromey MP, Vice Chair APPG for the Environment, House of Commons

In my time as a trade unionist and Member of Parliament for Erdington, I have seen tremendous change. Though there is much to applaud, the fact is that goods we consume are as likely to be produced thousands of miles away and not locally. This has led to a profoundly damaging impact on the lives of those who, traditionally, would have found employment in businesses producing the items we use. Birmingham, which may claim to be a 'spiritual home' for the car, has suffered a marked decline in the production of vehicles.

Industrialisation, particularly the internal combustion engine, made Birmingham, the 'city of a thousand trades', the destination for many immigrants, including the Irish like my Mum and Dad, who secured employment and better futures for their families. However, the pollution created as a result of this has led to a legacy that harms the continued existence of many millions. Greenhouse gases that have created climate change are a clear and present threat. According to the World Health Organisation, much in the news because of the coronavirus pandemic, climatic change that's already occurred is estimated to result in over 250,000 premature deaths annually across the globe.

Without policies explicitly dedicated to dealing with the way in which our economy functions, we risk reaching a 'tipping point' of average temperature increase which will make life impossible for, potentially, many hundreds of millions of people in areas of the world in which survival is perilous. It is essential that we support policies explicitly intended to ensure the rapid reduction of greenhouse gases, particularly carbon, that have proven so detrimental to the environment. Collectively we can alter our own lives as part of efforts to create a greener society that will protect the earth for the long-term.

I am passionate in my belief that change is possible. However, as my experience as an MP for a constituency with high levels of inequality and poverty, it is crucial that any change is not just ambitious in the objective of dealing with climate change, but radical in creating opportunity for all. The contributions presented by authors in this book underline the argument that developing a greener economy will potentially improve the environment through production of goods and services that are less harmful and benefit the economy.

Equally important, developing an economy based on green principles in which pollution and waste are drastically reduced will offer much needed employment. As such, the potential for a green economy will collectively make life better in terms of prosperity that is based on improvement in the prospects of future generations but not, as hitherto has been characteristic of traditional orthodoxy, through destruction of the earth's precious resources and delicately balanced environment.

There is much to do and little time to achieve it before it's too late.

More about Bite-Sized Books

Visit the Bite-Sized Books bookshop